GW00542556

Judy Garland

Judy Garland

Paul Donnelley

HAUS PUBLISHING • LONDON

Copyright © 2007 Paul Donnelley

First published in Great Britain in 2007 by Haus Publishing,
26 Cadogan Court, Draycott Avenue, London SW3 3BX
www.hauspublishing.co.uk

The moral rights of the author have been asserted

A CIP catalogue record for this book is available from the British Library

ISBN 978-1-904950-81-3

Typeset in Adobe Garamond Pro by MacGuru Limited
Printed and bound by Graphicom in Vicenza, Italy
Jacket illustrations: Getty Images

For Stacey Upson, with love

Contents

Foreword

The Judy Garland story is anything but straightforward. Even though historically she was born comparatively recently, much myth and misinformation have already entered the Garland lore. Supposedly respected biographers give different versions of tales. Was Judy's stage début an accident or was it planned? Names are consistently spelled in different ways. Were her sisters called Jimmy and Suzy or Jimmie and Suzie? Such is the troubled path that the new biographer must warily navigate.

I thought I knew a fair amount about Judy but when I began research in earnest I was shocked by the stories I learned. The way that Judy was used and abused by MGM is truly terrible. In 2007 movie stars go to extreme lengths to protect their public images – loving couples that really hate each other are careful not to let their animosity become public knowledge. Homosexual leading men marry willing women to hide their true natures lest their careers be harmed by the truth. Prima donnas employ press agents to show them in a favourable light and not as the egotistical maniacs that they really are. However, these are nearly always all personal choices. The young Judy Garland did not have choices – her decisions were taken away from her. Her mother – yes, her *mother* – began feeding her pep pills to keep her awake so that she could perform with her sisters. The studio forced her to take slimming pills to keep her weight down; forced her to take sleeping pills, uppers and downers so that she could work. The studio cafeteria was under strict instructions to feed the growing girl only chicken soup. Louis B Mayer refused to let her attend her high school prom and sent her on a promotional tour instead. Unsurprisingly, Judy's mother Ethel, an archetypal stage mother if ever there was one, was a party to this scandalous behaviour.

Judy sought love and affection wherever she could – often with disastrous consequences. She was regularly attracted to or became involved with the wrong men, men who saw her as a meal ticket.

Ultimately, the Judy Garland story is a sad one but her legacy lives on through her films and music. And that is something we should all be grateful for.

Paul Donnelley
www.pauldonnelley.com

Acknowledgments

I would like to thank Marie Ahsun for her interest in this project and for lending me a rare DVD about Judy.

Thanks are also due to the following: Sarah Bastow, Jeremy Beadle, Melanie Bissett-Powell, Emma Jones, Suzanne Kerins, Jo Knowsley, Annabel Laister, Nigel Lewis, John McEntee, Dominic Midgley, Louise and James Steen, Mitchell Symons, Catherine Townsend, Shannon Whirry, Liz Williams, Nicola Wilson, my agent Chelsey Fox and, of course, the beautiful Stacey Upson to whom this book is dedicated.

Chapter 1

Listen, Darling

Film star. Singer. Cabaret performer. Gay icon. An Academy Award winner. The wife of an Academy Award winner. The mother of an Academy Award winner. Who could know that the little girl born to Frank Gumm and his wife Ethel Milne at 5.30 a.m. at Itasca Hospital in Grand Rapids, Minnesota, on 10 June 1922 weighing seven pounds would be all this and much more? Dr H E Biner delivered the screaming infant.

The Gumm family was among the first settlers in Tennessee and a village was named in their honour. Francis Avent Gumm, Judy's father, was born in Murfreesboro, not far from Nashville in Tennessee on 20 March 1886. He grew to be a 5ft 11in[1] good-looker with a tenor voice and, although Judy would later claim that he was of Irish stock, in fact he had German, Scotch and French ancestry.[2] He was the third of William Tecumseh (1859–1906) and Clemmie Gumm's five children: Mary (1880), Robert (1883), William (1889) and Allie (1892). Frank was also homosexual. On 13 June 1899 he went to Sewanee Military Academy (later called the University of the South) to study business administration but he believed that he had show business in his blood

1

and in 1904 left the world of academia for the itinerant life of a vaudevillian. It also allowed him to indulge in his homosexual predilections although he often left towns very suddenly when his sexual approaches were rebuffed. 'Everybody in Superior was talking about it. I had no idea that there was anything like that going on', said Maude Ayres who had worked with Frank in the theatres.[3]

Judy's mother, Ethel Marion Milne, was born in Marquette, Michigan, on 17 November 1893. She was the eldest of eight children of John Milne and Eva Fitzpatrick. As well as a love of music, Ethel's mother instilled a self-belief in her daughter that was unshakeable. Eva was a typical stage mother and, like mother, like daughter, Ethel was to push her daughters onto the stage with fearsome enthusiasm. Ethel left school when she was just 11 years old and by the time of her 12th birthday she was a keen singer and piano player but unfortunately did neither particularly well. Nonetheless, she landed a job playing the piano in cinemas and in late 1913 she met 27-year-old Frank Gumm at the Princess Theatre in Superior, Wisconsin.[4]

They fell in love and were married in Superior on 22 January 1914. The Gumm family believed that Frank had married beneath himself – they had after all founded a village in the state of Tennessee. Minnie Gumm, Frank's aunt, commented, 'I always liked his little wife – but, you know, she was a Northern girl.'[5]

Frank and Ethel began a double act in vaudeville and their bill matter listed them as 'Jack and Virginia Lee, Sweet Southern Singers'. Their act had a bizarre beginning. The curtain would open and Ethel would be sitting demurely at the piano before Frank walked on and said, 'Good evening ladies and gentlemen. My name is Jack Lee and this is Virginia Lee, my wife' at which point Ethel would stand and bow to the audience. Frank continued, 'Virginia Lee will now open our programme by playing *Alexander's Ragtime Band*. I would like you all, please, to observe how small her hands are' and then Ethel faced the audience and showed them her hands. [6]

On 5 March 1914 the couple was hired to run the New Grand Theatre on Pokegama Avenue, one of two cinemas in Grand Rapids, Minnesota. (It had opened on 28 January 1914.) Frank would manage the establishment and sing while Ethel played the piano. But they missed their lives on the road and persuaded the owners to let them tour in the winter months. Ethel fell ill with the flu, however, and by 20 February 1915, just two months after their departure, they were back in Grand Rapids. It was when they returned that Ethel found that she was pregnant. On 24 September, Ethel gave birth to their first child, a daughter that they named Mary Jane although she changed her name to Suzy. Another daughter, Dorothy Virginia, known as Jimmy, was born on 4 July 1917. (It seemed a Gumm family trait that almost everyone changed his or her given names. Elizabeth Gumm, Frank's invalid mother who was born in 1857 and died aged just 38 in October 1895, preferred to be called Clemmie. His daughters Mary Jane, Virginia and Frances became respectively Suzy, Jimmy and Judy.)

Frank and Ethel realised that with two small daughters they would be unable to tour but it did not stop them performing in nearby towns and villages. The Gumms saved as much of their earnings as they could and bought a half share in the New Grand. In the summer of 1917, a future medical student called Marcus Rabinowitz (who would later change his name to Marc Rabwin), who was earning some money in his summer holidays selling films, travelled to see Frank and sold him several movies. The two men became firm friends and Rabinowitz stayed with the Gumms while he travelled to neighbouring towns and villages selling his films. Fearing interference from her mother-in-law and the end of her career if they stayed in one place, Ethel begged her husband to go back on the road. When he refused, she threatened to leave him. This was when women's emancipation had taken a hold in America. Then she discovered she was pregnant for a third time.

It was a difficult time and in November 1921 Frank went to see Marcus Rabinowitz, then in his second year of medical school at the University of Minnesota, and asked him to arrange an abortion. Rabinowitz refused to help, telling Frank that an abortion could be fatal for Ethel or cause serious medical complications.[7]

Persuaded by Marcus Rabinowitz, the Gumms decided to go ahead with the pregnancy. By the due time of the birth in late May 1922 the Gumms were expecting a boy, hoping for a boy and wanting a boy. Their daughter arrived nearly a fortnight after the due date but the advertisement in the *Grand Rapids Independent* still announced the birth of Francis Gumm, Jr. The baby girl was baptised Frances Ethel Gumm by the rector Robert Arthur Cowling at the Episcopal Church at 10 a.m. on 19 July 1922. Her godfather was Ted Toren and the godmothers Jenny Toren and Mrs Arnold Wickman. Frank Gumm was disappointed that his wife had given birth to a third daughter but Frances soon became his favourite and he called her 'Baby'.

'Baby' Gumm suffered a number of childhood illnesses and was often beset with earache. Ethel had heard a tale that hot salt was curative so she filed two of Frank's socks with salt, put them in the oven until they were hot and then hung them over Baby's ears. Judy recalled, 'I'd sit on the couch in the living room with those socks full of hot salt over my ears – I looked like a cocker spaniel most of the winter'.[8] Judy later put a gloss on her illnesses. She said, 'The beginning of my life was terribly happy … [Grand Rapids was] a magnificent-looking town … [our home was] everything that represents family: clean, old-fashioned, beautiful, not frightening, and a gay, good house. [The] only time I saw my parents happy [was] in that wonderful town.'[9]

Baby was, it seemed likely, destined like thousands of others to grow up in Grand Rapids and marry a local boy and raise a family. Whoever thought that reckoned without Ethel's determination. She longed for glamour and glitz in her life. She was an avid reader of tabloids and the burgeoning fan magazines and watched her cinematic heroes on the screen at her husband's picture house while her mother-in-law minded the children. Ethel also strayed several times from her marriage vows. Frank was dependable and steady, which in Ethel's eyes made him boring. Mrs Gumm may have been a romantic and a fantasist but she was also realistic enough to know that she did not have what it took to become a star. Her next best option was to transfer her ambition to her daughters. She persuaded Frank to put on a live act every Saturday to attract patrons. Ethel worked out a routine for Susie and Jimmy, then eight and five.

Sadly for Ethel, The Gumm Sisters did not thrill the patrons but she had faith in her daughters. On a cold Boxing Day 1924 Baby, then two and a half, was added to the act. The curtains opened and the two elder Gumm sisters began singing *When My Sugar Walks Down the Street* before a third voice was heard. Baby appeared, having been hidden by her sisters. The trio sang three numbers before Baby was left alone on the stage. She sang *Jingle Bells*, to the crowd's delight, and at the end instead of bowing and gracefully leaving the stage Baby sang the song again and again … and again. Finally, Frank motioned for his mother-in-law, Eva

Child stars were popular in Hollywood at the time and innumerable actors had 'Baby' prefaced to their name such as LeRoy Winebrenner who, as Baby LeRoy, appeared opposite W C Fields in *It's A Gift* (1934). Fields was so irritated by his co-star that he spiked his orange juice with gin. Baby LeRoy retired when he was four. Others included Baby Peggy, the Shirley Temple of her day, who wrote a book called *Whatever Happened to Baby Peggy*, and Baby Sandy who retired, like Baby LeRoy, aged four.

Milne, to take Baby off. The audience loved the performance and clapped and cheered.

It was also to Ethel's delight and she immediately put Baby into the act on a permanent basis and on New Year's Day 1925 she made her début proper. Ethel began booking her daughters into other towns. The professional career of Judy Garland had begun and she was not yet three years old. Ethel was determined that Baby should become a star and it was not long before the Gumm family home and the New Grand Theatre were up for sale as Ethel strove to make her dream come true. Frank's protests were brushed aside and the family set off west, playing any venues that would have them. Often they found that work was hard to come by. Thanks to the new-fangled attraction of the cinema, the music halls were closing down and the venues reopening to show films. The family performed and slept in cheap boarding houses or, if money was short, in their car. Frank opened the act singing *I Will Come Back* (many years later, this would be the number with which Judy Garland ended her weekly TV show); Ethel played the piano and, after the girls had performed, closed with a song. Ethel always moved the audience. Unfortunately, she moved them because she was so bad. On occasion, the audience would boo and throw food at her. The crowd's hostility to her mother was something that the adult Judy Garland would always remember. Sometimes the Gumms would perform before a film was shown. It was not always a popular distraction. They would also have to be wary of the Gerry Society, a child protection organisation that enforced child labour laws, which forced the girls to attend school for a week if they came to its attention. The girls did not mind but Ethel was furious because it meant her dream was once more delayed.

With her mother busy preparing a bid for stardom and her

sisters much older than her, Baby became still more attached to her father. She felt annoyance and jealousy when her mother upset Frank or became angry with him. One reason for her rage was his drinking. Despite Prohibition being in force in America at the time, Frank always managed to get his hands on a bottle of Irish whiskey. It was as if the alcohol salved his feelings of emasculation.

It was not just Ethel's ambition that necessitated a move away from Grand Rapids. Frank had once again been behaving inappropriately towards young men. He spent a night with the star of the local high school baseball team, albeit, it would appear, with the permission of the boy's parents. It was when he made sexual advances to the male ushers at the New Grand Theatre that it was suggested that it would be best for everyone if he were to leave town. On 8 June 1926 they set off for California. The family arrived in Los Angeles in July and returned to Grand Rapids on the 18th of that month only to pack. (By 1926 Marcus Rabinowitz, now Marc Rabwin, was chief resident at Los Angeles County Hospital.) They had no accommodation booked and the girls were asleep, Frank exhausted. The story is told that Ethel insisted that they immediately begin visiting the sights and dragged her family to Grauman's Chinese Theatre. With Baby in her arms she marvelled at Sid Grauman's picture place and woke her daughter to show her the magnificent building. Judy Garland's first glimpse of Hollywood was thus one of its famous landmarks. Unfortunately, the facts do not bear out the legend. The Gumms arrived in Hollywood in the autumn of 1926 but Grauman's Chinese Theatre at 6925 Hollywood Boulevard, Central Hollywood, did not open until 19 May 1927. It is possible they went to the Egyptian Theatre at 6712 Hollywood Boulevard which had opened on 18 October 1922 with the gala première of *Robin Hood* starring Douglas Fairbanks.

The Gumms found some rooms and Ethel began preparing for her youngest daughter's big break. She sewed dresses, teased hair and ensured that Baby was fully rehearsed. There were no talking pictures so Ethel ensured that Baby was able to project her personality visually. Leaving her husband and elder daughters at the boarding house, Ethel set off to do the rounds of the studios. If Ethel thought breaking into the film world would be easy, she was quickly disavowed of the notion. She was ill prepared for the long queues of other mothers and moppets, the rudeness of the casting directors and the doors being slammed in her face. Speaking to some of the other mothers she learned that Baby's chances would be enhanced if she had an agent. Equipped with this new knowledge, Ethel and Baby made the rounds of agents but she encountered the same queues, the same rudeness and the same slammed doors.

For once Frank stood up to his wife and in May 1927 the family moved to Lancaster, a small town 80 miles north of Los Angeles and 2,350ft above sea level, where on 21 May he invested what was left of the family savings in the local cinema, the Antelope Valley Theater on Antelope Avenue. Baby and her sisters attended the Antelope Valley Joint Union School. Then Baby again fell seriously ill with the complaint (possibly acute acidosis) that had so affected her in Grand Rapids, Minnesota, in September 1925. Breaking the rules (under California law Baby was not eligible because she was not a charity case), she was admitted to the Los Angeles County Hospital where Baby was treated by Dr Oscar Reiss, who would go on to found the Reiss-Davis Child Study Centre in Los Angeles in 1950. Baby was dehydrated and feverish but thanks to the care of Doctors Reiss and Rabwin, she pulled through and was back at school by September 1927.

Stability in a small town was not part of Ethel's plan. Her

marriage was beginning to come under strain (she obviously knew of her husband's sexual predilections) and she contacted the cousin of a friend from Grand Rapids. The cousin was Laura Gilmore and soon Ethel, Laura, Frank and Laura's husband, an engineer called Will, would go out as a foursome. As time passed Frank began to spend more time on his business and neglect his wife while Laura was incapacitated by a stroke. It was not long before Ethel and Will Gilmore were lovers. Judy was to write later, 'A terrifying man. I loathed him. He had very white teeth, very bad clothes, a miserable haircut, and he was a petty, weak man, narrow-minded and unkind.'[10]

A good portion of Frank's time was spent not attending to his working life but his sexual one. He would often sit in the back row of the cinema with one of his young boyfriends for a spot of mutual masturbation. He also regularly gave oral sex to high school athletes but they usually forced him to beg before they would let him. Oddly, although it appeared that Frank's sexuality was an open secret among the local boys, none of them thought to tell their parents about Frank's activities. The reason was simple: they liked Frank and did not want to cause him any trouble.[11]

Ethel also had her daughters to concentrate on and so every weekend she drove the three girls the three-hour journey to Los Angeles in search of fame. To keep the girls alert she gave them pep pills and when they could not sleep Ethel casually handed her daughters sleeping pills. In late 1927 she enrolled her daughters in Mrs Meglin's School of the Dance in Los Angeles.[12] A subsidiary was the booking agency Meglin's Kiddies and Ethel took every job they offered. The Gumm Sisters played fêtes, lunches, fayres and even one whole evening for just 50 cents. Ethel hoped that in the audience might be that talent scout who would recognise

Frances's potential – or that friend or relative of the scout who would pass on the good news that a new star was in the offing.

Frank's business acumen had not failed him and he bought two more cinemas. Meanwhile, Ethel came to the realisation that instead of helping their sister the presence of Suzy and Jimmy was actually harming her, detracting from her appeal. The two elder girls would in time be dropped from the act and Baby became a solo artiste. Sometimes Baby was booked for a series of shows that meant she and Ethel had to be on the road for a week at a time.

It was around this time that the inferiority complex that would plague Judy Garland all her life was born. Baby was a chubby child with awkward mannerisms. Her contemporaries on the scene were invariably slim and seemingly poised. Ethel was of little help. She saw Baby not as a daughter but as a means to an end. She expected maturity beyond her years. In fact, Ethel was often cruel to her daughter. If her daughter was understandably upset at being dragged to yet another strange town and sulked, Ethel would slowly and deliberately pack her suitcase and tell Baby that she was leaving her because she was bad. Baby begged Ethel not to leave her but her pleas were ignored and she would leave, locking the door behind her. Baby by this time was hysterical and she was left alone until Ethel decided that she had been punished enough. When she returned to the room, Baby would beg for her forgiveness. Baby was younger than most of the other children and retreated into her own world, playing with her dolls, all of whom she called Peggy. Baby began to resent her mother for pushing her and taking her away from her beloved father. Baby was alone. On the road she was alienated from the other children by her age; at home her sisters were at school and other children ignored her because their mothers told them that stage children were beneath them. She was to say later, 'I was always lonesome.

The only time I felt accepted or wanted was when I was onstage performing. I guess the stage was my only friend, the only place where I could feel comfortable. It was the only place where I felt equal and safe.'[13]

The Gumm sisters appeared in the Meglin Kiddies Show at Loew's State Theatre on 22 December 1927 and Baby impressed everyone who saw the show with her rendition of Sophie Tucker songs.[14] From August 1928 they appeared on *The Kiddies Hour* on Los Angeles radio station KFI. The sisters spent from 11 until 13 June 1929 appearing in a Mayfair Pictures Corporation short film called *Starlet Revue*. Judy had spent the days after her seventh birthday in front of a camera. That same year the girls also appeared in three Warner Bros Vitaphone short films (*A Holiday in Storyland*, *The Wedding of Jack and Jill* and *Bubbles*). In October 1929 the Stock Market crashed in New York and millions were ruined. President Herbert Hoover – the first Chief Executive to have a telephone on his desk in the Oval Office – refused to help. Yet whatever their personal circumstances it seemed that Americans still found the money, albeit a few cents, to go to the cinema – enjoying a few hours' respite from their troubles. Thus the Gumms were not obviously short of money because Frank's chain of cinemas continued to pull in the crowds. However, the money being poured in did not always match the return coming out and it dried up when the town became aware of Frank's peccadilloes and stopped patronising the Valley Theatre. A whispering campaign began and one that was not quite so silent. 'The rumour killed him in the community. People kept mouthing about it and mouthing about it, and it just ruined his career here,' remembered W M Redman, a friend of Frank.[15] Eventually, Frank had to give up the lease on 1 April 1935 as he was unable to meet the rent.[16]

Baby's career continued apace. By the time of her tenth birthday Frances – the Baby tag had been dropped – had blossomed into an awkward pre-teen devoted to her father, disliking her pushy mother and a keen collector of stray dogs. Ever inconsiderate of her daughter's feelings, Ethel moved her into a hotel, the Hotel Gates, from where she would continue her assault on Hollywood.

The Gumm sisters enrolled at Mrs Lawlor's School for Professional Students[17] in Silver Lake and while there Frances met a boy called Mickey McGuire who had appeared in more than 50 short films. They quickly became close friends and would in time appear in 10 films together after he became Mickey Rooney and she Judy Garland. Rooney was able to make his new friend laugh and he became a welcome relief to the quarrels that beset her home life.

In 1933/4 Chicago played host to the World's Fair called the Century of Progress Exposition. Among the attractions were an eight-acre Hall of Science that showed how civilisation had grown in the area since 1833, a reconstruction of a Mayan temple and a dancer called Sally Rand who appeared naked apart from two large fans. The Century of Progress Exposition attracted 38.6 million visitors. Among them were Ethel Gumm and her three daughters. In June 1934 they got a job – unpaid – on a theatre on the Midway. Gangsters ran the establishment and none of the acts received any financial reward. If any complained they soon found their employment terminated. Few did complain, this being only five years after the St Valentine's Day Massacre when seven members of the Bugs Moran gang were murdered by four of Al Capone's lieutenants.[18] Frank had given Ethel some money so she was perhaps not quite as dependent as the other performers. As always, she also hoped that one of the many visitors might

Mickey Rooney was born Joe Yule Jr in Brooklyn, New York on 23 September 1920. He began his showbiz career when he was just 15 months old. In 1926 he made his film début in *Not To Be Trusted* playing a midget! Between 1927 and 1933 he appeared than 50 silent comedy shorts. In 1934 he signed to MGM and played Andy Hardy in 15 films. His career tailed off when he returned from serving in the Second World War. Rooney has appeared in more than 250 films in a career spanning 80 years. He has been married eight times and has fathered nine children.

An early photograph of Judy Garland (standing, far right) at a party for child actors in Hollywood in 1931

13

be a talent scout. After three months the money ran out but Ethel's pride refused to let her call Frank for help and when she went to the management of the theatre to ask for their unpaid wages, she was promptly sacked. Desperate, she traipsed around every theatre begging for work before striking lucky at the Oriental Theatre where the entertainer George Jessel was headlining. The Oriental wanted Frances and not her sisters but Ethel had not prepared a solo act so they took all three on the proviso that Frances was featured heavily.

On the opening night, 17 August 1934, they stood outside the theatre looking at their names up in lights but their pride turned to anger when they saw themselves listed as 'The Glum Sisters'.[19] At various times they had been billed as 'The Crum Sisters', 'The Dumb Sisters' and even 'The Rum Sisters'.[20] Jessel suggested they adopt the name of the *New York World-Telegram* theatre critic Robert Garland[21] and Frances went one further by taking as her Christian name the title of her favourite song of the time *Judy* by Hoagy Carmichael. Ethel did not agree and suggested Babe[22] but Jessel and the management stood firm and Judy Garland was born. That night he introduced 'The Garland Sisters – featuring Little Miss Judy Garland with the big voice'.

The sisters earned enough money to return to Los Angeles and after four months apart Judy was reunited with her beloved father. The car pulled into the driveway at three in the morning and Frank ran out to greet his family. Judy later recalled, 'I cried out of happiness and that was a first too. It's hard to explain but all the times I had to leave him, I pretended he wasn't there; because if I'd thoughts about him being there, I'd have been too full of longing.'[23]

The next year was spent again visiting studios and receiving yet more knockbacks. They made an appearance in an MGM

Ethel Gumm's fussier influence, on her daughter Judy's appearance, can be seen in this early portrait in 1935

19-minute short, *La Fiesta de Santa Barbara*, billed as The Garland Sisters. They were booked into venues close to home so they could continue their education at Mrs Lawlor's. They spent two summer seasons at the Cal-Neva Lodge on Lake Tahoe.[24]

The tales of how Judy came to the attention of MGM are, to say the least, mixed. Marc Rabwin, by now married to Marcella Bennett, David O Selznick's executive secretary, threw a party to which he invited Joseph L Mankiewicz. Judy sang at the party and Mankiewicz was so impressed he mentioned Judy to Ida Koverman, Louis B Mayer's right-hand woman. A childless widow, she preferred to be known as Kay.

During their second season at Cal-Neva the Garland sisters encountered the Hollywood agent Al Rosen. Stories vary as to what happened. Rosen claimed that he asked Judy to go back into the lodge's casino and, while she was there, he asked her to perform the song *Dinah* for himself, owner 'Bones' Remer, songwriter Harry Akst and Twentieth Century-Fox talent scout Lou Brown. Ethel and the girls waited in the car. In another version the sisters were on their way home when Jimmy remembered leaving a box of hats and their musical arrangements in their dressing room. Reluctantly, Ethel turned the car around and when they got back to the lodge she sent Judy to collect them. Judy bumped into 'Bones' Remer who introduced her to Akst, Rosen and Brown. In all innocence she asked Akst to play *Dinah*, little knowing that he had written it. Judy did not know how to read music so she was told to begin singing and Akst would fall in with her. She was nervous. She had never sung without Ethel being present. She was also fearful of her mother's reaction if Ethel found out what she was doing. Despite all this, she impressed the men but Lou Brown was convinced that she would not be any good for films. Al Rosen disagreed and gave Judy his number, telling her to have her mother call him in a few days when he was back in his Los Angeles office. The journey home was almost over before Judy told Ethel about the audition. To her amazement her mother was calm.

Or was Ethel present at the audition? Did she say within Judy's earshot, when asked by Akst why Judy was not in films, 'I think it's because she just isn't pretty enough'?[25]

However the situation arose, Al Rosen became Judy's first agent although he refused to represent her sisters and insisted that Judy work with another arranger and not her mother. It was a tricky situation for Judy. She was pulled between two people – both of whom had her best (professional) interests at heart, both of whom hated each other and both of whom saw her as a meal ticket. It was no surprise that Judy became an emotional wreck in later life. Rosen took her to a cantor to improve her voice before the trek around the studios began once more. Moreover, once again the reaction was the same: no. They all agreed that Judy's singing voice was incredible but could not see a future in films for a chubby, not especially pretty 13-year-old. Judy was not helped by the fact that her mother still dressed her as a cutesy baby, all ruffles and curls in her hair.

Rosen rang on the afternoon of 13 September 1935 to tell Judy to get over to MGM[26] immediately. Ethel was out shopping so Frank took his daughter to the studio. Luckily, Judy was dressed very casually in jeans, trainers and a dirty shirt and not in the clothes her mother usually put her in. Frank played for his daughter but Ida Koverman was not impressed by his virtuosity and summoned Roger Edens (who was to become her future musical mentor)[27] to play the piano. Judy sang *Zing! Went the Strings of My Heart* and Koverman called Louis B Mayer. Mayer watched without emotion and when Judy had finished he got up and left without saying a word. For a fortnight they heard nothing from the studio, then word came. Without so much as a screen test MGM wanted to sign 'little Judy Garland'.

Chapter 2

A Star is Born

Louis B Mayer (?1885–29 October 1957) was born in Dymer in the Ukraine. Mayer bought the Orpheum, an old cinema in Haverhill, Massachusetts in 1907 and by 1914 owned the largest chain of picture houses in New England. In 1916 he left to become a movie producer, creating his own company Louis B Mayer Pictures. On 17 April 1924 his company merged with Metro and Goldwyn Pictures. For some time films were released as 'A Metro-Goldwyn Picture, Produced By Louis B Mayer' until at Mayer's insistence the name became Metro-Goldwyn-Mayer. Mayer was appointed General Manager and Vice President, a rôle he would hold until 25 July 1951 when he lost a power struggle to Dore Schary.

MGM was dominated by the tiny presence of Louis B Mayer. He was the wealthiest and most powerful of the movie moguls. It was Mayer's vision that made the studio one of the most successful in the 1930s. Mayer spent the most to hire the best and was amply rewarded himself, becoming the highest-paid person in America. Mayer ran MGM like a family, rewarding loyalty and punishing those who didn't have the company's best interests at heart. Screenwriter Herman J Mankiewicz said, 'He has the memory of an elephant and the hide of an elephant. The only difference is that elephants are vegetarians and Mayer's diet is his fellow man.' He had an on-off relationship with his production chief David O Selznick who was also his son-in-law. A rabid Republican, Mayer had been instrumental in the foundation five years earlier of the Academy Of Motion Picture Arts & Sciences.

Judy's MGM contract was signed (by Ethel, for Judy was a minor) on 27 September 1935[28] and officially started four days later. Her starting salary was $100 per week with options for seven years. The seven years worked out as follows: Year One: 6 months at $100 per week with a 20-week guarantee of work; 6 months

at $200 per week with a 20-week guarantee; Year Two: $300 per week with a 40-week guarantee; Year Three: $400 per week with a 40-week guarantee; Year Four: $500 per week with a 40-week guarantee; Year Five: $600 per week with a 40-week guarantee; Year Six: $750 per week with a 40-week guarantee and finally, in Year Seven she would earn $1,000 per week, again with 40 weeks of work guaranteed.

Judy entered the happiest time of her life. She was spending quality time with her beloved father, her mother was content because her daughter was signed to the biggest studio and her dream of stardom was almost realised, and her sisters were happy because they did not have to perform anymore. It was to be a painfully brief respite.

On the night of Friday 15 November 1935 Frank Gumm complained of an earache. After taking quinine tablets he continued to feel unwell so was taken to Cedars of Lebanon Hospital at 1.40 p.m. on the Saturday. The next day Frank Gumm died of spinal meningitis at 3 p.m. It was Ethel's 42nd birthday. Unbeknown to the family Frank had arranged a surprise birthday party for Ethel, and many guests, unaware of the tragedy, turned up in high spirits only to have them crushed amid much embarrassment. Judy was to say many times in the coming years, 'My father's death was the most terrible thing that ever happened to me in my life.'[29] The loss would stay with her for the rest of her life. Many years later, she told her daughter Liza, 'I thought "Now there is no one on my side".'[30] She could not cry at Frank's funeral at Forest Lawn's Little Church of the Flowers in Glendale and was ashamed by this. For the next eight days Judy was morose, melancholy and tearless. It could not go on and on the ninth day she locked herself in the bathroom and cried and vomited for 14 hours. Ever unsympathetic, Ethel insisted Judy tidy herself up and go to the

The King of Hollywood, Louis B Mayer looks upon the world from his desk at Metro Goldwyn Mayer

studio. When she arrived she was told Louis B Mayer wanted to see her. It would be the first time he had spoken to her. He offered Judy some sympathy and then told the terrified girl, 'I am your father and whenever you have trouble and whenever you need anything come to me and I will help you.'[31]

Judy was to say, 'When Dad died MGM took over as my father. In our house the word of Louis B Mayer became the law. When Mother wanted to discipline me, all she had to say was "I'll tell Mr Mayer".'[32] For many years speculation has arisen exactly what the relationship was between Judy and Louis B Mayer. It is known that he had a penchant for young girls and while he was apparently never explicit in his demands it was implicit that young ladies who denied him had potential careers ruined. Judy was 14 when she fell into his orbit. One story has it that he would often summon her to his office where he would fondle her breasts. Mayer said that Judy sang from the heart and would place his hand on her breast to show where her heart was. Judy was to comment, 'I often thought I was lucky I didn't sing from another part of my anatomy.'[33] He ignored her complaints and invited other MGM execs to follow his lead. For almost 17 years Judy 'belonged' to Louis B Mayer – she virtually lived and breathed MGM and when the studio demanded she jump, she would only pause to ask how high. Judy was to remark that she was uncertain just how altruistic Mayer's motives were. 'Metro thought they were raising me. They were just dreadful ... They had a theory that they were all-powerful and they ruled by fear. What better way to make young persons behave than to scare the hell out of them every day? That's the way we worked ... that's the way we got mixed up. And that's the way we lost contact with the world.'[34] Frank's death had left the Gumms dependent on Judy and her $150-a-week salary (minus Al Rosen's 10 per cent). Frank left just $256 in cash and a $150 stock certificate. Ethel once again put her own wishes before her daughter's and threatened Judy every time she misbehaved that she would inform Mr Mayer. For most of the 1930s there were no child labour laws and children's income belonged to their parents. Judy signed over her pay packet to her mother for the next five years, perhaps expecting her mother to put aside some of the income as a nest egg for Judy. But since Judy realised what her mother was like, perhaps she knew that Ethel would have no qualms about spending money that morally was not hers.

Judy spent a lot of time with Deanna Durbin and her friend Mickey Rooney while all three waited for their big break. Louis B Mayer ordered that Judy be slimmed down and when she went to the studio commissary no matter what she ordered she was given only chicken soup. She attended exercise classes and practised singing with Roger Edens. MGM decided that it had no need of Judy and Deanna Durbin so both girls were put in a two-reel short film directed by Felix Feist to see who would be kept and who let go. The film is variously known as *Every Sunday*, *The Sunday Afternoon* or *Every Sunday Afternoon*. Mayer was in Europe while the test was shot. Upon his return he and several of his executives watched the film and Mayer asked which girl should be kept. The view was split so Mayer decided to keep them both and ordered that they be cast in a musical together.[35] It was then discovered, however, that no one in the legal department had thought to renew Durbin's contract and she had been signed by Universal to appear in Joe Pasternak's *Three Smart Girls* (released on 1 January 1937 and made on a budget of $326,000) opposite Ray Milland, Binnie Barnes and Alice Brady. The Henry Koster-directed film made her an international star overnight. A sequel was later made, *Three Smart Girls Grow Up* (released 24

On 4 May 1939 the California State Assembly recommended passage of the Child Actor's Bill – commonly know as the Coogan Act – to protect young performers and ensure that at least 50 per cent of their income was set aside for them. The child actor Jackie Coogan earned more than $4 million and was told by his parents that they were putting a large percentage of that money into a trust for him. When he reached his majority, he learned that there was no trust fund. His father was dead and his mother had married his business manager, Arthur L Bernstein. His contract with MGM over, he sued his mother and stepfather and managed to get $126,000 but five years of court battles used up most of that amount.

March 1939). With Deanna Durbin's stardom and regular rôles for Mickey Rooney, it seemed that Judy was being left behind. Twentieth Century-Fox's Darryl F Zanuck asked Mayer if he would lend him Judy for a film to be called *Pigskin Parade* and Mayer agreed.

Less than a year after her contract with MGM was issued, Judy signed a recording contract with Decca Records. On 12 June

1936, just two days after her 14th birthday, she recorded *Stompin'* *at the Savoy/Swing Mr Charlie* with Bob Crosby and His Orchestra for Decca in New York. They were the first Judy Garland songs ever to be released.

In August 1936 Judy began work on her first feature film. She played Sairy Dodd and filming took a month. *Pigskin Parade* (released 23 October 1936) starred Stuart Erwin, Patsy Kelly, Jack Haley, Johnny Downs, Betty Grable, Arline Judge, Dixie Dunbar, Tony Martin and Elisha Cook, Jr and had Alan Ladd in a bit part as a student. Directed by David Butler, the critic Leonard Maltin described the film as an 'entertaining college football musicomedy with Erwin the [yokel] who becomes a gridiron hero'.[36] When Judy sang *It's Love I'm After* to Tony Martin, cast and crew broke professional decorum and clapped on set.[37] Frank S Nugent of *The New York Times* mentioned Judy in his review, 'In the newcomer category is Judy Garland, about 12 or 13 now, about whom the West Coast has been enthusing as a vocal find … She's cute, not too pretty, but a pleasingly fetching personality, who certainly knows how to sell a pop.'[38] Judy was not impressed, however, by her own performance. 'I was frightful, I was fat – a fat, little pig in pigtails. My acting was terrible. It was just little Kick-the-Can Baby Gumm – just dreadful.'[39]

On 1 February 1937 Louis B Mayer hosted a party on the set of the film *Parnell*. Judy sang *Dear Mr Gable/You Made Me Love You* to Clark Gable on whom she had a crush. Mayer was sufficiently impressed by the rendition that he had Judy sing the song to a photograph of Clark Gable in *Broadway Melody of 1938* (retitled from *Broadway Melody of 1937*!). It was filmed between February and 20 July 1937 and released on 20 August 1937) in which she played Betty Clayton. The scene captured hearts the world over and Bosley Crowther wrote in *The New York Times*, 'There are

Judy's close friend in her early days in Hollywood was Deanna Durbin. Seen here with Eddie Cantor in a photograph taken by Alfred Eisenstaedt in 1938. Her early and meteoric rise to fame would briefly eclipse Judy's. By the 1950s she had abandoned show business, for a closely guarded and happier personal life

individual successes in the film … the amazing precocity of Judy Garland, Metro's answer to Deanna Durbin … Miss Garland particularly has a long tour de force in which she addresses lyrical apostrophes to a picture of Clark Gable. The idea and words are almost painfully silly – yet Judy … puts it over – in fact with a bang'.[40] *The Hollywood Reporter* was equally enthusiastic. 'The sensational work of young Judy Garland causes wonder as to why she has been kept under wraps these many months. She sings two numbers and does a dance with Buddy Ebsen. Hers is a distinctive personality well worth careful promotion.'[41] Then she appeared playing Cricket West opposite Mickey Rooney in the horseracing comedy drama *Thoroughbreds Don't Cry* (released 25 November 1937). The film was shot between September and 13 October 1937 and was originally intended to star Freddie Bartholomew but he was unavailable because of a custody battle between his parents and his aunt. Ronald Sinclair was cast as Roger Calverton in his place. Roger came to America with his father Sir Peter (C Aubrey Smith) to race. Rooney played Timmie Donovan, a jockey, and Judy was the niece of Aunt Edie Ralph (Sophie Tucker) the owner of the boarding house where the jockeys stayed. It was the first time that the two friends had appeared in a film together.

In a world where egos are, to say the least, fragile, actors tend to be pampered and indulged. No such luxuries were afforded Judy. At home she was called Baby, Monkey or Pudge and at the studio Mayer referred to her as 'My little hunchback'. Being surrounded with gorgeous and sexy women every day, even if they did not have one tenth of Judy's talent, did not help her self-esteem. Mayer summoned her to his office and ordered her to stop cheating on her diet. She would visit ice cream parlours to indulge in her favourite sundaes but would always be spotted by MGM spies who would report their findings to Mayer. Mayer

Judy and Buddy Ebson, in a scene from 'Broadway Melody', the film that would bring her to the attention of the critics and the studio chiefs

sent her to the studio doctor who gave her a diet pill. The tablets worked but had the unfortunate side effect in giving Judy insomnia. There was no problem that the MGM medics could not fix and Judy was given Seconal to help her sleep. Judy was just 14 years old and her lifelong battle with drugs that had begun some years earlier with her own mother would now be an imposing presence in her life until her death. The chicken soup and diet pills made Judy faint and so it was suggested that she needed more sleep. Unbelievably, on the days she was shooting Judy was given a large dose of Nembutal to put her to sleep and then 15 minutes before she was due in front of the cameras she was woken up and given a dose of uppers to get her alert and able to work.

'The early days at MGM were a lot of laughs. It was all right if you were young and frightened – and we stayed frightened. Look at us – Lana Turner, Elizabeth Taylor, Mickey Rooney, and me – we all came out of there a little tricky and kooky' was Judy's verdict on her days at the studio.[42] MGM dictated what Judy ate and wore and who she saw. She was terrified of Mayer and Ethel and just one person seemed to be in her corner and that was her musical mentor Roger Edens. He encouraged her and comforted her and she trusted him completely, knowing that he would never let her down and he never did. Edens was not able to instil a fighting spirit in Judy – he consoled her when she felt down but could not give her the confidence or the advice to prevent the blows landing in the first place.

The next project Judy worked on was *Everybody Sing* and Judy received top billing with Allan Jones and Fanny Brice. The film began shooting on 2 September 1937 and wrapped on 21 December 1937[43] with retakes for two days from 8 January 1938. The 91-minute film was released on 4 February 1938. A modern critic lambasted it as a 'shrill musical with stupid plot [and] unmemorable songs'.[44] The original title was *The Ugly Duckling* but unfortunately the film did not turn into a beautiful swan, although Judy managed to rise above the dross and give a strong performance. Around this time Al Rosen pulled a stroke that consolidated Ethel's position despite his antipathy towards her. He arranged for her to be hired as Judy's 'coach and manager' at a salary of $200 a week. It drove a further wedge between mother and daughter because Ethel's first loyalty was now not to her daughter but to Louis B Mayer. On 24 May 1938 Judy was involved in a car crash and broke three ribs, as well as spraining her back and puncturing a lung but she was back in the studio by 11 June.

Judy was assigned to star opposite another successful child star, Freddie Bartholomew, in her next film, *Listen Darling*. Costume tests took place on 28 June 1938. The film also starred Mary Astor, Alan Hale and Walter Pidgeon and featured superior material to *Everybody Sing*. Judy performed a number of songs including *Zing! Went the Strings of My Heart*, *Nobody's Baby*, *On A Bumpy Road to Love* and *Ten Pins in the Sky*. Mary Astor played a single mother for whom Judy and Bartholomew tried to find a husband. Frank Nugent, the reviewer for *The New York Times* wrote, 'The comedy has been nicely turned out by Mary Astor, Walter Pidgeon, Alan Hale, Gene Lockhart and Charley Grapewin, among the adults, and by all three youngsters. Besides being a charming little miss, Judy Garland has a fresh young voice which she uses happily on *Zing! Went the Strings of My Heart*, *On a Bumpy Road to Love*, and *Ten Pins in the Sky* ... It is really a natural, pleasant and sensible little film.'[45]

Meantime, Mickey Rooney was rapidly moving up the MGM star rota playing Andy Hardy and in the 1938 *Motion Picture Herald* popularity poll he was third behind Clark Gable and

Shirley Temple. Mayer realised that Judy's star was also in the ascendancy and he wanted her to appear with his biggest boy star, so she was cast in *Love Finds Andy Hardy* (1938). In this, the fourth in the series, Judy played Betsy Booth who was visiting the Hardys' next door neighbours. Andy was not smitten with Betsy until he heard her sing. But even then his aesthetic appreciation of her did not stop him being torn between her, his high school sweetheart Polly Benedict (Ann Rutherford) or the local bad girl Cynthia Potter (Lana Turner). *Love Finds Andy Hardy* was not one of the best of the series and the action was constantly slowed down so as to allow Judy to sing, the sole reason she was in the film in the first place. Despite this, the audience was much taken by the chemistry between Judy and Rooney and word went out to find more starring vehicles for them. MGM believed that Garland and Rooney could be another Nelson Eddy and Jeanette MacDonald, Fred Astaire and Ginger Rogers or Wallace Beery and Marie Dressler.

Mickey was the first boy that Judy fancied but she was upset and not a little jealous when he went out on dates with other girls, all of whom were, in Judy's insecure eyes, sexier or more glamorous than her. Things were no better at the studio where she mixed with beauties such as Lana Turner, Ava Gardner,[46] Hedy Lamarr, Greta Garbo, Myrna Loy, Claudette Colbert, Luise Rainer *et al*. Although blessed with talent, Judy did not have the two characteristics that she equated with sex appeal: a curvy figure and long, lustrous hair. Judy stood just 4ft 11½in and had a tendency to put on weight, so she would starve herself which did not help her health or her hair.

Chapter 3

Everybody Sings

Songwriter Arthur Freed was a young man in a hurry. He had written the lyrics for *Singin' in the Rain*, *I Cried for You* and *You Were Meant for Me* but he wanted more. Whenever he saw Louis B Mayer he would ask to be allowed to direct a film but Mayer always found ways to circumvent Freed's ambition. Finally, Mayer told Freed to find a project and then, maybe, he would consider allowing him behind a camera. Freed looked in MGM's archive but nothing was suitable but someone mentioned a property written by L Frank Baum and then owned by Samuel Goldwyn. Freed saw potential in *The Wizard of Oz*, which was more than Goldwyn did, and, more presciently, he saw Judy in the rôle of Dorothy Gale. Freed began secret negotiations with Goldwyn and bought the rights. Mayer agreed with Freed that it was a good property but refused to countenance letting Judy play Dorothy. The film, Mayer decided, would star Shirley Temple, then under contract to Fox. He summoned Freed to his office and told him the news. Freed was to be associate producer. The plans hit problems when Fox refused to loan Temple. Back to Plan A and Judy was told the rôle was hers. She was also told to

lose weight and put on a special diet. Richard Thorpe was hired to direct and Harold Arlen and E[dgar] Y[ipsel] 'Yip' Harburg to write the score.

At this time Ethel also manoeuvred Al Rosen out of the picture. Judy and Ethel were earning $350 a week with Ethel earning $50 more than her daughter. Mayer had a secret meeting with Ethel and persuaded her to sign with his friend Frank Orsatti, a bootlegger and pimp-turned-agent. Orsatti 'arranged' for a pay rise of $150 to placate Ethel. In comparison, Mickey Rooney who had a good agent was then earning $5,000 a week.

MGM threw all their resources into *The Wizard of Oz*. Judy was more concerned with her education. When the film wrapped on 16 March 1939 she would graduate from Hollywood High School. At least that was the plan. It was customary then that when child actors reached school leaving age they would enrol in a local school for a few days before the end of term and then graduate with the class. Judy could not attend the day school at the studio and was assigned a tutor, Rose Carter, who was with her for eight hours a day. Whenever Judy was not in front of the cameras she was being tutored.

Filming began on 13 October 1938 but according to Margaret Hamilton, who played Miss Almira Gulch/the Wicked Witch of the West, it was not a happy set. The four male principals – Bert Lahr (Zeke/Cowardly Lion), Ray Bolger (Hunk/Scarecrow), Jack Haley (Hickory/Tin Man) and Frank Morgan[47] (Professor Marvel/Emerald City doorman/taxi driver/Wizard's minder/Wizard of Oz) – were worried that Judy would upstage them and played not with her, but against her. Hamilton was horrified to learn that Judy was on drugs to cope with her hectic schedule.

The main thing that excited Judy during filming was the thought of graduating and she proudly showed Margaret

The role that would define Judy for the rest of her life. Dorothy Gale in 'The Wizard of Oz'. She is seen here in a publicity still with cast members; Jack Haley, Bert Lahr, Frank Morgan and Ray Bolger at the door of the Emerald City. 1939

Originally, Ray Bolger was the Tin Man and Buddy Ebsen the Scarecrow in *The Wizard of Oz* but Bolger insisted on swapping parts because his childhood hero Fred Stone had played the Scarecrow on stage in 1902. Ebsen then had to drop out when he had a severe allergic reaction to the make-up used for the Tin Man. Le Roy then sacked the director Richard Thorpe and scrapped the first week's footage. George Cukor stood in as director until Victor Fleming took over. On 4 November Jack Haley was hired to replace Ebsen as the Tin Man although it is Ebsen's voice that you can hear on the soundtrack.[48]

Hamilton the dress she intended to wear. However, when filming was over Judy was sent on a tour with Mickey Rooney and never got to graduate in the dress. Margaret Hamilton telephoned the publicity department to protest only to be told that Louis B Mayer had expressly ordered the tour.

Yip Harburg remembered, 'Here was Dorothy a little girl from Kansas, a bleak place where there were no flowers, where there was no colour of any kind. What does a child like this want? The only colourful thing in her life was a rainbow.'[49]

In fact, the song nearly did not make it into the final film. It was thought *Somewhere Over the Rainbow* was too cloying and too sentimental and was dropped from the final edit. It was put back into the film after a sneak preview revealed that the film was rather slow and needed to quicken the pace and also because it was too late to compose another number.

The film was a spectacular in more ways than one.[50] Seven assistant directors worked on the picture and 15 people contributed to the final script. All of MGM's 29 sound stages were used for the 65 sets and the cast finally numbered 600. The budget ran to $2.78 million, an unheard-of figure for that time but the first weekend's takings were $5.35 million. Judy was to say later, 'I think the American people put their arms around me when I was a child performer, and they've kept them there – even when I was in trouble.'[51]

After the previews MGM began to realise that they had potentially a massive hit on their hands and in Judy a huge star. However, for some reason the studio did not treat Judy with the respect that was her due. They insisted that she was only a success because of them and sent her on a cross-country tour (the one Margaret Hamilton tried to block) with Mickey Rooney, telling Judy that they hoped some of his talent and charisma would rub off on her. It was unforgivable behaviour. *The Wizard of Oz* premièred at Oconomowoc, Wisconsin, on 12 August 1939 followed by premières in Hollywood three days later and in New York at the Capitol Theatre at 51st Street on 17 August 1939.

Rewarding Arthur Freed for his success on *Oz*, Mayer gave him a budget of $748,000 to make Judy's next film, a Rodgers & Hart show called *Babes In Arms* (1939) in which she played Patsy Barton. Mayer involved Busby Berkeley in the production and with him came the Freed Unit comprising Roger Edens, choreographer Chuck Walters, musical director Georgie Stoll, art director Cedric Gibbons, cameraman Ray June and scriptwriter Fred Finklehoffe. The team was known as 'the fairy unit' because of the number of homosexuals who worked on it. The Freed Unit (apart from Finklehoffe who did only three) worked on the four big musicals that starred Garland and Rooney – *Babes In Arms*, *Strike Up The Band*, *Babes On Broadway* and *Girl Crazy*. All, apart from *Babes On Broadway*, were based on successful Broadway shows.

Babes In Arms was in production between 12 May and 18 July 1939 and Judy played someone her own age – 17 as opposed to an 11-year-old in *The Wizard of Oz*. The film was basically a starring vehicle for Rooney with Judy playing an important but small rôle as the plain girl who worships Mickey Moran (Rooney).

Judy was once again back on the filmmaking treadmill. Having finished the tour, she made *Babes In Arms* and then 12 hours after that wrapped she began filming *Andy Hardy Meets Debutante* (1940), reprising her rôle as Betsy Booth. When that production was over she was shunted to the sound stage to make *Strike Up The Band* (from 19 April until 16 July 1940). It was a schedule that would have exhausted the fittest man alive and so it was unsurprising that insecure Judy could only cope by the studio feeding her drugs. 'They had us working days and nights

Mickey Rooney looks on, as Judy sets her signature into wet concrete outside Grauman's Chinese Theatre in Los Angeles

on end. They'd give us pep pills to keep us on out feet long after we were exhausted. Then they'd take us to the studio hospital and knock us out cold with sleeping pills – Mickey sprawled out on one bed and me on another. Then after four hours they'd wake us up and give us the pep-up pills again so we could work 72 hours in a row. Half of the time we were hanging from the ceiling, but it was a way of life for us',[52] Judy told *McCall's*. Ever protective of Judy, Roger Edens complained to Arthur Freed about the appalling treatment but Freed was helpless to do anything because the orders were coming directly from Louis B Mayer.

The premiere of *Babes In Arms* was at Grauman's Chinese Theatre at 6925 Hollywood Boulevard, Central Hollywood on 10 October 1939. Judy was invited to join the ranks of Hollywood stars by leaving her mark in the wet cement outside the cinema. Judy knelt besides the cement and wrote *For Mr Grauman, All happiness, Judy Garland, 10-10-39* before pressing her handprints into the wet mix. Unbelievably, Ethel leaned over her daughter and with her own finger straightened a letter in Judy's signature. Even on this day the ghastly Ethel could not help but interfere in her daughter's life.

Judy was exactly four months past her 17th birthday and her anxieties, insecurities and lack of confidence were at their apex. For a star of her magnitude her salary was a pittance – just $500 a week and 40 per cent of that went to Ethel. Her romantic life – such as it was – was organised by the studio. Dates were not for her benefit but to keep her name in the public eye. Her education was lacking – Roger Edens would discuss music and musicians with her but Judy was too embarrassed to admit she had little or no idea what he was talking about – and her schedule was such that she had no time to visit libraries to teach herself. For many contract players their mundane backgrounds were jazzed up to

Theories abound as to how the tradition of stars leaving their hand and/or footprints in the cement outside Grauman's Chinese Theatre started. One version has it that Norma Talmadge visited the construction site of the theatre and accidentally stood in some wet cement, inspiring Grauman with the idea of a permanent record of celebrities. Another story has it that Talmadge, Douglas Fairbanks and Mary Pickford arrived for a visit and it was Pickford who stepped in the cement. Grauman himself provided two more versions. He accidentally trod in some wet cement and the idea struck him. Alternatively, Grauman was told off as a child for ruining some wet cement and this was his adult revenge.

make them more exotic and interesting but Judy was afforded no such hyperbole.[53] Her story was recounted as it had happened.

In December 1939 Judy confided a secret in one of her close friends, Barron Polan. She would, she told him, leave show business when her contract expired and become a writer. She even had a book of her poems printed privately, which she presented to Polan. She never confided her dream to Ethel who would no doubt have called the idea foolish and unworkable.

Again Judy and Mickey Rooney found themselves relying on the other for moral support. 'Work and fun were inextricably interwoven,' said Rooney. 'It was impossible to tell where one ended and the other began. Our work was our fun and our fun was our work.' Around this time Ethel regularised her relationship with Will Gilmore. Knowing how close Judy was to her father, was it another slap in the face that Ethel and Gilmore were married in Yuma, Arizona on 17 November 1939, the fourth anniversary of Frank's death? 'That was the most awful thing that ever happened,' recalled Judy. 'My mother marrying that awful man the same day my daddy died.'[54] Was Ethel callous or merely unthinking? When they married Gilmore moved into the house and Judy began plotting to leave.[55]

Chapter 4

Thoroughbreds Don't Cry

On 29 February 1940 Judy and Mickey Rooney were among the star-studded audience as Bob Hope emceed the Academy Awards broadcast live on the wireless from the Cocoanut Grove in the Ambassador Hotel. Rooney had been nominated for Best Actor for *Babes In Arms* while Judy was presented with a special Oscar in recognition of her outstanding performance as a screen juvenile. 1939 was the year of David O Selznick's *Gone with the Wind*. It won nine Oscars – Best Film, Best Director, Best Actress, Best Supporting Actress, Best Script, Best Colour Cinematography, Best Art Director, Best Editing and a special award for use of colour. Clark Gable playing the dashing Rhett Butler lost out as Best Actor (as did Rooney) to Robert Donat for his brilliant performance as the shy but dedicated schoolmaster Charles Chipping of Brookfield School in *Goodbye Mr Chips* (1939). Judy also performed the winning song *Somewhere Over the Rainbow*. If one looks at a picture of the winners that night Judy looks gauche and ill-at-ease, as if she is a youngster who has been allowed to stay up past her bedtime but then finds it difficult to cope with the grown-ups. At the after-show party Judy became very friendly

with Tyrone Power, who recognised the woman in the girl's outfit. Mayer was furious that his portrayal of Judy as the all-American girl would be wrecked if she was seen to be romancing an older, sophisticated man. Mayer sent out word to his pet journalists that nothing was to be written of the burgeoning affair. Judy's first grown-up romance soon ended – it would be perhaps the only time in her life that she felt loved and beautiful.

On 9 March 1940 the West Los Angeles Police Department received an anonymous telephone call informing them of a plot to kidnap Judy. A 19-year-old man was arrested and confessed that he and an older man intended to hold Judy for a $50,000 ransom. The older kidnapper was still at large and the police put armed guards on Judy's house. Terrified, Judy telephoned Tyrone Power and he immediately came to her aid, driving her to the relative safety of Tijuana. Unfortunately, in doing so Power put himself at risk of breaking the Mann Act (transporting a minor across state lines for immoral purposes). When Ethel learned where her daughter was and with whom, she ordered the couple back to California. On their return, Power began dating the glamorous Lana Turner. If Power had wanted to harm Judy's already fragile self-esteem, he could not have done a better job than by hooking up with the sexy, beautiful Turner – everything that Judy believed she wasn't. The elder potential kidnapper was never found and Judy's life returned to as normal as was possible for someone in her situation. Work became even more intense and Judy's insomnia increased. Her body had become accustomed to the pills she was given and so she could no longer be knocked out and awoken with uppers and downers. Judy's home life was no better – Ethel continued to interfere in every aspect and Judy had no privacy.

On 12 March 1940 Judy appeared on the Bob Hope radio

Judy and Mickey Rooney captured in an energetic publicity shot for 'Babes in Arms'

41

David Rose (15 June 1910–23 August 1990) was born in London but his parents emigrated to the United States in 1914 and he was educated at the Chicago College of Music. In 1929 he began working for NBC Radio. Nine years later, he formed his own orchestra. In 1941 Rose began working in films and wrote compositions for almost 40 movies. He was nominated for an Oscar for *So In Love* from the Danny Kaye film *Wonder Man* (1944). He later moved to television and he spent 14 years writing music for *Bonanza* and ten for *Little House on the Prairie*. One of his most celebrated compositions was *The Stripper* which he wrote in 1962.

show and there she met David Rose who was conducting the orchestra. Rose spoke to Judy about music and she fell in love. They began dating in earnest but also in secret.

Judy had told a fan magazine that she had no interest in the opposite sex. 'Nobody thinks less about boys than I do. I don't want to get married until I'm 24. Why 24? Well, that sounds like a good while away.'[56] This statement was entirely disingenuous – not only was Judy desperate to get married but she had been sleeping with various men for some time. She had lost her virginity by the time she was 15. She had been romantically linked with Freddie Bartholomew, Jackie Cooper, Billy Halop, Frankie Darro and Buddy Pepper. She had a serious but platonic relationship with Oscar Levant, the composer, and a similar fling with the musician Artie Shaw. Then came a passionate affair with the songwriter Johnny Mercer in April 1940.

On 10 June 1940, Judy's 18th birthday, she posed with Ethel and Louis B Mayer for publicity to mark her milestone. Later that day Rose gave her an engagement ring and the couple announced their intention to marry. Not surprisingly, Mayer was furious. It was made worse, in his eyes, because Rose was a former beau of Jeanette MacDonald whom Mayer himself had once romanced. On 26 June Judy received her high school diploma from Los Angeles's University High School.

At this time Judy left home, although Mayer insisted that she live with a chaperone. A young woman who had befriended Judy agreed to share with the teenage star. She also changed agents at this time, signing with Leland Hayward after Barron Polan, by this time a former MGM employee, persuaded Ethel that Frank Orsatti was ripping off Judy. Hayward paid $25,000 to buy out Judy. Judy was then paid $500 a week by the studio but she was allowed to keep the money paid to her by radio shows. Mayer fought back. On 26 September he offered Judy a seven-year contract worth $2,000 a week for three years, $2,500 a week for years four and five and $3,000 a week for the final two years with a guarantee of 40 weeks' work a year. In total Judy would be paid $680,000 over seven years. Ethel and Judy went to the Los Angeles Superior Court to have the contract validated. That evening in her home Judy and Rose planned a secret elopement. The next day the couple was summoned to Mayer's office where he forbade them to marry under threat of Rose being blacklisted from every studio and radio station. Judy's flatmate, far from being her friend, was a studio spy and she betrayed the lovers to Louis B Mayer. The couple agreed to wait a year before marrying.

Meanwhile, Rose was shocked by Judy's punishing work schedule and did what he could to protect her but, as many others discovered, he was powerless to stand up to the might of Louis B Mayer. Rose could not even control Judy's diet. At Mayer's insistence Judy had only chicken soup, black coffee, 80 cigarettes a day to curb her appetite and pills every four hours. Judy said, 'I swear there must have been a vat full of chicken soup at the MGM commissary with my name engraved on it. If I sneaked in for a chocolate sundae with pecan nuts and bogs of whipped cream on top – I used to dream about those things – I would always get the same story: "Sorry Mr Mayer has left instructions about what you are to eat today – chicken soup".'[57] Rose composed their song *Our Love* and he played it as often as possible on his wireless shows. Judy became convinced that everything would be fine once she and Rose became man and wife but in the meantime she relied ever more heavily on the studio's medicine cabinet. The dieting kept her 4ft 11½in frame at a steady seven stone but it also left her permanently hungry.

In *Strike Up The Band* (1940) Judy played Mary Holden to both public and critical acclaim. The film, which was made on a budget of $839,000, was filmed between 19 April and 16 July 1940 and once again teamed Judy and Mickey Rooney. It was the tale of Jimmy Connors and his girlfriend who want to appear in a school music contest but they cannot afford the fare.

On her 18th birthday in June 1940 Judy's salary was increased to $2,000 a week for three years, $2,500 a week for the next two years and $3,000 a week for the final two years of her new contract which was signed on 28 August 1940. Although Judy was an adult she was still, legally, a minor and Ethel also signed 'as mother of artist'. Judy and Ethel also agreed privately that Ethel should go on the payroll on a salary of $125-a-week.

In her next film, a musical called *Little Nellie Kelly* (1940), which was budgeted at $665,300, and in which she played the title rôle, Judy received her first screen kiss.[58] Judy was also permitted to grow up in her last outing with Andy Hardy, *Life Begins for Andy Hardy* (1941) which was filmed between May and 27 June 1941. It is generally regarded as one of the better vehicles in the series.

Growing up also meant getting married and Judy believed that the marriage to David Rose would be a panacea for all her problems. Others were not so sure. Leland Hayward tried to talk Judy out of marriage and suggested she and Rose live together. Although Hayward was de facto her agent, this suggestion caused a huge rift between them and Judy specifically asked for Barron Polan to exclusively represent her. When filming wrapped on *Life Begins for Andy Hardy*, Judy had a few days' grace before she began rehearsing for *Babes on Broadway*. Judy had wanted a big traditional church wedding but more than that she wanted to be Mrs David Rose. Remarkably, Ethel put her daughter's personal

The happy couple, Mrs and Mr Rose. Judy poses on a garden seat with her first husband, bandleader David Rose in 1941

happiness above concern for her career, possibly for the first time in her life. She told a friend, 'If I don't let her marry Dave, she'll always say, "Well if you had let me marry him, I might have had some happiness".'[59] At 1 a.m. on Monday 28 July 1941 Judy and David Rose were married in Las Vegas, Nevada. Within 24 hours the studio became aware of the ceremony and Judy was ordered back to the studio for work on *Babes on Broadway* – no honeymoon for the newlyweds. *Babes on Broadway* wrapped on 15 October 1941.

The first marital home was the Ambassador Hotel.[60] In October 1941 they moved into a house at 10693 Chalon Road in Bel Air. David Rose's hobby was model trains and he had a vast collection that sprawled around the grounds. Although miniature, the trains were large enough to take passengers. Ethel hired a couple as housekeepers and although Judy paid their wages, they reported to her mother. Judy had wanted to be married but even in her own home, she played second fiddle to her housekeepers who treated her like a child and when she looked out at the garden she saw 1,000ft of railway track to accommodate her husband's hobby. To top it all, Judy then discovered she was pregnant. She waited for some time before telling her husband and mother. Her husband was less than enthusiastic at the thought of impending fatherhood and her mother, once again, thought of Judy's career. She would be able to complete *Babes on Broadway* without a bump showing but Judy was signed to make *For Me and My Gal* immediately afterwards.

Ethel took matters into her own hands, as she always did. She visited Arthur Freed who was producing *Babes on Broadway* and would also helm *For Me and My Gal*. Further meetings were arranged with other studio executives and it was decided that the best thing would be for Judy to have an abortion. The fact that abortion was then illegal in California and that Judy would have to have the termination *sub rosa* did not seem to unduly worry the MGM executives nor Ethel. Someone who was worried was Judy but her best interests were never paramount. David Rose was of little help so Judy turned to Barron Polan but he was too young to give any real advice and so the

MGM studio doctor performed the termination in a Hollywood hospital. The studio press office announced that Judy had suffered from a problem with her tonsils. Forty-eight hours after the operation Judy was back at home and a further 48 hours after that she was in MGM's recording studio dubbing work on *Babes on Broadway*. The film cost $940,068 so there was no way that anything as minor as an abortion was going to stop the studio making Judy work.

Many women feel guilt at terminating a baby and Judy was no different. She blamed herself. She was not strong enough to stand up to her mother. She was not strong enough to stand up to the studio. She did not love herself. If only she had had the strength, the will, but she didn't. She was not forced to have the abortion. She signed the forged documentation. She had not been kidnapped or drugged. She could not forgive herself, so how could she forgive others, including her husband. For a year after the operation Judy tried to keep her marriage alive but she found herself falling out of love with her husband. Yet she feared divorce because she was scared it would once again deliver her to the less-than-tender mercies of her mother and the studio. In truth, she had never really escaped from their power. She was also fearful that David would be drafted into the army, although his status as a married man allowed him some leeway. Barron Polan was the first of her male friends to join the army.

Filming began on the Busby Berkeley-directed *For Me and My Gal*[51] on 3 April 1942 and the film was budgeted at $802,000. Casting was a laborious process. The studio had to find an actor who was talented enough to play Harry Palmer, to be able to sing and dance well. But he also had to be believable enough to sacrifice his vaudeville partner for his career and maim his own hand rather than serve in the First World War. Many of the

Busby Berkeley (29 November 1895–14 March 1976) was born in Los Angeles as William Berkeley Enos. He was nicknamed 'Busby' after Amy Busby, a *fin de siècle* Broadway actress. He moved into movies, choreographing *Whoopee* (1930) at the behest of Samuel Goldwyn and then went on to work on *Palmy Days* (1931), *Roman Scandals* (1933), *42nd Street* (1933) (for Warner Bros), *Gold Diggers Of 1933* (1933), *Footlight Parade* (1933), *Dames* (1934), *Gold Diggers Of 1935* (1935), *Stage Struck* (1935), *Gold Diggers Of 1937* (1936), *Gold Diggers In Paris* (1938), *Men Are Such Fools* (1938), *Bitter Sweet* (1940), *Take Me Out To The Ball Game* (1949), *Call Me Mister* (1951), *Million Dollar Mermaid* (1952) and many more. It was his undoubted genius that saved the company from going under. Yet he never had a day's dance lesson in his life.

MGM contract players balked at the thought of playing such a part, fearing it would harm their chance of stardom.

David O Selznick had recently signed a promising youngster by the name of Gene Kelly and he was flown from Broadway to audition for the rôle. However, Kelly's screen test was appallingly bad and Selznick dropped him. It was Judy who believed that Kelly would be perfect for the part of Harry Palmer. He was born in Pittsburgh, Pennsylvania, in 1912 and studied economics at university before deciding to concentrate full-time on show business. Judy went to see Busby Berkeley and Arthur Freed to persuade them to cast Kelly. They watched the screen test again but it did not improve with a second or third viewing. Kelly sat for the executives and took more tests and Judy pushed for him. Finally, they agreed to cast him as Harry Palmer. The film, even seen today, is a moving experience. Kelly plays the part with more naïveté than villainy and at the end he and Judy are reunited for their starring performance at the Palace Theatre. Filming ended on 23 May 1942. The reviews were favourable although they noted Judy's skinny frame. Writing in the *New York Daily News*, Kate Cameron opined, 'Judy looks thin and frail throughout the picture but she seems to have developed enormously as an actress and entertainer since her last screen assignment.'[62] *Time*'s critic wrote, 'Bony-faced Judy Garland is already well-graduated from a sort of female Mickey Rooney into one of the more reliable song pluggers in the business.'[63]

Gene Kelly went on to star in *Du Barry Was A Lady* (1943), *The Cross Of Lorraine* (1943), *As Thousands Cheer* (1943), *Christmas Holiday* (1944), *Anchors Aweigh* (1945) for which he was nominated for an Oscar, *Ziegfeld Follies* (1946), *The Pirate* (1948), *The Three Musketeers* (1948), *Black Hand* (1949), *Take Me Out To The Ball Game* (1949) which he also choreographed, *On The Town*

(1949) which he also directed, *Summer Stock* (1950), *An American In Paris* (1951), *It's A Big Country* (1951), *The Devil Makes Three* (1952), *Singin' in The Rain* (1952) which he also directed, *Brigadoon* (1954) which he also choreographed, *The Happy Road* (1957) which he also directed, *Les Girls* (1957), *Marjorie Morningstar* (1958), *Let's Make Love* (1960), *Inherit The Wind* (1960), *Viva Knievel!* (1977) and *Xanadu* (1980). He also directed *Hello, Dolly!* (1969). Kelly was awarded a special Oscar in 1951 'in appreciation of his versatility as actor, singer, director and dancer, and especially for his brilliant achievements in the art of choreography'. He died in 1996 after a long illness.

Judy was in the Top 10 Box office stars; she was well paid; she had public adoration and critical acclaim but she was not happy. Her mother and stepfather had taken over management of her career and were investing her money. She was estranged from her husband. Judy was ill but she was intelligent enough to realise that her malaise was not just a physical one, it was psychological as well. She went to see her friend Joseph L Mankiewicz who recommended Karl Menninger, a psychiatrist he knew. Menninger, in turn, put Judy in touch with his associate Dr Ernst Simmel and Judy began secret 45-minute sessions with him before going to work. When Mayer learned what was happening he called Mankiewicz into his office and told him to mind his own business. Mankiewicz was furious at what he saw as Mayer's callousness and offered his resignation, which Mayer refused to accept. He did, however, not use Mankiewicz for quite some time until the writer quietly left for Twentieth Century-Fox. Instead of relaxing the chain he kept Judy on, Mayer tightened it, making her schedule even more demanding. He did not understand or refused to understand that Judy was mentally ill and that it was caused by the regime he insisted she followed. Judy and David

Rose announced their separation in the last week of January 1943 and divorced the following month with the decree absolute on 8 June 1944. The sexually adventurous Judy was later to tell friends that the reason the marriage ended was because Rose had called her 'despicable' when she suggested he perform cunnilingus on her.[64] To others she was more circumspect, saying that 'He acts like an old man'.[65]

Following her separation from Rose Judy began to see Tyrone Power, then married to the French film star Annabella, once again and she also had a lesbian relationship with Betty Asher,[66] her publicist.[67] Asher who was described by one of Judy's biographers as 'a slim, sad, unattractive girl'[68] had had an affair with Artie Shaw, after telling his then girlfriend, Lana Turner, that she was better off without him. Asher then went to see the musician. 'The next thing I knew we were in bed together,' remembered Shaw.[69] Whether she performed the same service and bedded Turner is unknown. Asher was also the girlfriend of studio honcho Eddie Mannix.

The next person to occupy Judy's bed was Joe Mankiewicz and Judy fell for him heavily, even calling him the love of her life. There was never any chance that he would marry her, not least because he was already married.

Six years previously, Joe Pasternak had tried to hire Judy for a Universal film called *Three Smart Girls*. Now he was on the Metro lot to film the Booth Tarkington novel *Presenting Lily Mars* (1943) beginning on 3 August 1942. Lily Mars (Judy) was an aspiring singer who wanted to appear in a new play being produced by John Thornway (Van Heflin). The original idea had been to film the book as a drama with Lana Turner but Pasternak preferred to make a musical and cast Judy. 'She had,' he recalled, 'a small child-like quality, pathetic, making you want to hug and cuddle her. She admired Lana and no convincing could make her believe she was anything other than second choice – a replacement. It took her a long time to appear from make-up. She thought she was ugly. The singer and actor Mario Lanza had some of the same problems.'[70]

Although Pasternak praised Judy both to her face and behind her back, she never felt especially comfortable with him. She was unable to unburden herself, to take him into her confidence. He added, 'I prayed for her. I saw what might happen and I prayed. Such a great talent. She deserved God's personal attention.

'She was not too glamorous for the girls to dislike her or be jealous of her, and she was beautiful enough for the men to fall in love with her. Those eyes – when she looked at you! She sold herself to everybody individually and collectively. You believed everything she did.'[71]

Her confidence for once buoyed by *Presenting Lily Mars*, Judy asked Mayer if the studio would allow her some time off to appear on stage. Mayer merely laughed at her and cast her opposite Mickey Rooney in *Girl Crazy* (1943) which began shooting on 4 January 1943 with a budget of $1,140,850. Judy played Ginger Gray. If *Presenting Lily Mars* had given her a self-belief and a glimpse into what she would like to do, she was brought down to earth during the filming of *Girl Crazy*. She no longer laughed at Mickey Rooney's attempts to make her smile and she was unamused by him trying to make her fluff a line by behaving like a 'tic-ravaged chimpanzee' behind the cameraman. His practical jokes left her cold, literally on one occasion when he woke her shouting 'Fire' and throwing a glass of water into her face. For the first time Judy fell out with a director. She fell foul of Busby Berkeley's perfectionism and was happier when he wasn't on set and Norman Taurog took over.

Off-screen, Judy was becoming a physical and emotional

The publicity and promotion of the Rooney-Garland film 'Girl Crazy' was relentless. The film went on to gross nearly four million dollars at the box-office in 1943

wreck – she was going through a nervous breakdown. She relied ever more heavily on pills – pills to wake her up, pills to send her to sleep; she had nightmares that her voice would break and her career would end; she feared silence and always had the radio on or made phone calls often during the bouts of insomnia that would plague her all her life; and she lost her dream house when the mortgage went unpaid.

Filming ended on *Girl Crazy* on 19 May 1943 and Judy asked her mother to go and see Louis B Mayer and have her admitted to the Menninger Clinic for six months. 'Father' knows best and once again Mayer saw himself as the omnipotent paternal figure in his stars' lives. He refused to allow Judy any time off and told her she was to appear in *As Thousands Cheer* (1943) and when that was finished she was to participate in a promotional tour. It was relentless. When *Girl Crazy* opened in America it took $3,770,000 at the box office.

At the Robin Hood Dell Theatre in Philadelphia, Pennsylvania in July 1943 Judy made her first concert appearance. André Kostelanetz conducted the 90-piece orchestra and Judy opened with four Gershwin songs before 36,000 fans. After the intermission Judy performed songs from her own films. When the concert, which was a great success, had finished, she said, 'I thought to myself that they were probably thinking what I was doing there anyway, so I just sang louder.'[72]

It was at this time that Judy's insomnia really took a frightening grip and she began making late-night telephone calls. Judy often rang Dr Simmel to talk things over but she was not always completely honest with him and often dreaded talking to him. She found it difficult to converse with the much older man. One night she decided she needed to talk to him to correct some of the things she had told him but as she attempted to reach him she washed down her Nembutals with vodka. When she finally got hold of him, he rushed over to her. Studio gossips referred to the incident as her 'first phoney suicide attempt'.

Now Mayer took action – he began searching the MGM lot for an arranged husband for Judy: she needed someone who

Vincente Minnelli (28 February 1903–25 July 1986) was born, as Lester Anthony Minnelli, in Chicago, Illinois, the grandson of an Italian revolutionary. He began his career as a window dresser and then became a photographer's assistant and then a costume designer. He had directed a number of stage shows and three films when he was given the chance to direct Judy. His films garnered 20 Oscars and included *Madame Bovary* (1949), *Father Of The Bride* (1950), *Father's Little Dividend* (1951), *An American In Paris* (1951), *The Band Wagon* (1953), *Brigadoon* (1954), *Kismet* (1955), *Lust For Life* (1956), *Designing Woman* (1957), *The Reluctant Debutante* (1958), *Gigi* (1958), *Four Horsemen Of The Apocalypse* (1961), *The Courtship Of Eddie's Father* (1963), *The Sandpiper* (1965) and *On A Clear Day You Can See Forever* (1970). He died aged 83 at his home in Beverly Hills.

could love her, reassure her, fulfil her sexually, and a man who was sensitive. Vincente Minnelli, a shy, unattractive, effeminate, cosmetic-wearing, inarticulate homosexual, beset by a tic, would not perhaps have been most people's first choice.

The Minnelli/Garland partnership really began on the set of the film *Meet Me In St Louis* (1944) in which Judy played Esther Smith. The movie, the highest-budgeted one Judy had appeared in, was based on a series of articles by Sally Benson that had been published in the *New Yorker*.[73] However, it almost never got made. Judy did not like Minnelli, she thought that he was overrated and he made her feel uneasy. But Mayer was insistent and threatened to suspend Judy if she did not work on the film. Production began on 10 November 1943 although filming didn't start until 7 December, two years to the day after Pearl Harbor. Her co-stars were Tom Drake (it was intended that Van Johnson play this role), Mary Astor, Leon Ames and Lucille Bremer. Minnelli was a perfectionist who insisted on shooting some scenes as many as 25 times. Judy loathed him and sought out the company of her leading man Tom Drake. Unfortunately, Drake was also gay but Judy took his inability to get an erection as a personal insult. When filming ended on 7 April 1944 it could not come too soon for Judy. Her view of her director changed, however, when she began looking at the rushes and saw that she was not just good, Minnelli had made her the best she had ever been. The *Los Angeles Times* lauded it as 'one of the Great American Family sketches' and the movie became a box-office smash. It was against this background that Garland fell in love with Vincente Minnelli. He had made her look stunning on film. She and Minnelli began to have dinner with Don Loper and then alone and romance blossomed. Not long after the film wrapped they began living together, Judy studiously ignoring the clues to Minnelli's true sexuality.

Meet Me In St Louis was a huge financial as well as critical success for MGM and once again the studio was keen to cash in on Judy's popularity. They cast her as Alice Mayberry in *The Clock* (1945) with Fred Zinnemann at the helm – it being thought that Minnelli was unsuitable to direct a drama. Zinnemann and Judy got on well but there was no spark between star and director and when he saw the rushes he knew that he was not the man for the job. Judy went to see Arthur Freed who agreed that the studio had been wrong to hire Zinnemann and on 23 August 1944 he was sacked. For eight days the film was directorless. Judy asked Freed to give the job to Vincente Minnelli but he was still unsure. Eventually, he gave in and on 1 September 1944 *The Clock* resumed shooting with Vincente Minnelli as director.

The Clock, which wrapped on 21 November, was a romance about two people who meet and fall in love in just 48 hours during the Second World War. Judy looked at herself on the big screen and for the first time in her life liked who she was. Again Minnelli had made her look good with help from wardrobe and make-up. It was a remarkable performance – Judy is alive sexually, something that happened rarely on screen or off in all her all too short life. She gelled with her co-star Robert Walker, who was beset with difficulties himself.

Walker was born in Salt Lake City Hospital, Utah in 1918, the son of an uncaring journalist father and a distant mother. In January 1935 he won an award as Best Actor in San Diego County for his performance in the play *The Other Side*. At the end of the year, he tried out for the American Academy of Dramatic Art in New York. He was accepted after auditioning five days after his 19th birthday. On 2 January 1939 he married the actor Jennifer Jones and they had two sons: Robert, Jr and Michael. Walker was hired for $25 to appear in the NBC radio soap opera

Yesterday's Children. That led to regular work in soaps. In 1941 the couple's happiness was wrecked when mogul David O Selznick took a very personal interest in Mrs Walker. On 9 December 1942 it was announced that Selznick had cast Jennifer Jones in *The Song Of Bernadette* (1944) and thus began his seduction of her in earnest. Walker was flourishing at MGM where he had made a name for himself in *Bataan* (1943). Audiences took to his look, due mainly to his inability to focus properly. As Jones became more and more ensconced with Selznick, Walker became more and more belligerent. MGM studio chief Dore Schary recalled: 'Bob began drinking and asserting his vigour and masculinity by going into bars and brawling with men who were bigger and hit harder.' Walker appeared in *Madame Curie* (1943), *See Here, Private Hargrove* (1944), *Since You Went Away* (1944) which featured several love scenes with his estranged wife, much to the distress of them both, *Thirty Seconds Over Tokyo* (1944), *What Next, Corporal Hargrove* (1945), *The Sailor Takes A Wife* (1946), *The Sea Of Grass* (1947), *Song Of Love* (1947), *One Touch Of Venus* (1948), *Vengeance Valley* (1951), *Strangers On A Train* (1951) and *My Son John* (1952). Walker and Jones were divorced on 20 June 1945. He hit the bottle with enthusiasm and was often arrested for drunken behaviour. Schary gave him the ultimatum of his career or booze. Walker was admitted to the Menninger Clinic where he stayed for eleven months. On 8 July 1948 Walker married Barbara Ford, the daughter of director John Ford. They separated five weeks later. Ford was granted a divorce on 16 December 1948 on the grounds of extreme cruelty. Rumours circulated that he had hit her and Ford's friends John Wayne and Ward Bond had to be restrained from beating up Walker. The actor knew what was wrong with him but was too scared to admit the truth. 'I basically felt inadequate, unwanted, and unloved since I was born. I

Louis B Mayer adds a paternal presence to Judy and Vincente Minnelli's wedding reception

was always trying to make an escape from life. I was an aggressive little character, but what nobody knew but me was my badness was only a cover-up for a basic lack of self-confidence, that I really was more afraid than frightening.'[74] Walker died at 9 p.m. on 28 August 1951 at his home 14238 Sunset Boulevard.

Meanwhile, the romance between Judy and Vincente Minnelli was becoming serious. On 9 January 1945 Minnelli and Judy announced their engagement. He had proposed at a restaurant called the Villa Nova at 9015 Sunset Boulevard in Hollywood.[75] Judy loved Minnelli because he made her look good on screen but also because she thought that he believed in her and would help her to break away from the musical niche in which MGM had placed her. Louis B Mayer approved of the romance because he knew that Minnelli would do no such thing.

The marriage took place on 15 June 1945 in Judy's mother's house and the ceremony was performed by Dr William E Roberts of the Beverly Hills Presbyterian Church (which Judy had never attended). Ira Gershwin was the best man and MGM chief Louis B Mayer took the paternal role in which he always saw himself anyway – he gave the bride away. The bride wore a pearl-grey jersey gown. Roberts held a wooden staff for the bride, groom, best man and matron of honour to grasp to show the solemnity of the marriage. Four hands took the implement and then a fifth appeared as Mayer grabbed the stick at the top. It seemed that there would be 'three in the marriage'. Mayer helped the couple to buy a sumptuous hilltop house. His behaviour was not entirely altruistic. He reasoned that the couple would not cause any problems that risked suspension because if they did they would be unable to meet the mortgage on their expensive home.

The Clock premiered on 22 March 1945 and received critical acclaim with *Time* lauding Minnelli's 'semi-surrealist juxtapositions, accidental or no, help turn *The Clock* into a rich image of a great city. His love of camera booms and dollies makes *The Clock*, largely boomshot, one of the most satisfactory flexible movies since Frederick Murnau's epoch-making *The Last Laugh*'.[76] Barely had the newlyweds time to catch their breath when Judy discovered by the end of August that she was pregnant.

Chapter 5

For Me and My Gal

The Minnellis' first and only child, a daughter, arrived by cæsarean section in Cedars of Lebanon Hospital, Los Angeles, at 7.58 a.m. on Tuesday 12 March 1946 weighing six pounds 10½ ounces. They named the little girl Liza May Minnelli for an Ira Gershwin song and Minnelli's mother. The singer Kay Thompson (who was Judy's lesbian lover) and Bill Spear were her godparents.

If Judy thought marriage to Minnelli and the birth of their daughter would assuage her problems she was in for a nasty surprise. Following Liza's birth Judy suffered from very severe postnatal depression and also developed genophobia (fear of sexual intercourse) – which was to stay with her for a very long time and might explain why, albeit subconsciously, she went on to marry homosexuals.

Judy was seriously ill and Minnelli and Ethel even discussed retirement but career if not wiser heads prevailed and after a few weeks' rest Judy was once again before the cameras. She appeared as Marilyn Miller in *Till the Clouds Roll By* (1946), a biopic of Jerome Kern directed by Richard Whorf.

On 21 November 1946 MGM gave Judy a new contract and

*Mother and daughter, Judy
with Liza Minnelli on the set of
'Words and Music' in 1948*

raised her salary to $5,619.23 a week for the subsequent five
years.

Judy's next film was *The Pirate* (1948), a film about mistaken
identities, to be directed by Minnelli. It was based on a play
written by S N Behrman for Alfred Lunt and Lynne Fontanne
and changes were made to facilitate Judy and Gene Kelly. It was

61

probably the most demanding part that Judy had undertaken. She had to dance, sing (including a powerful rendition of *Be a Clown*) and change character quickly. Minnelli said, 'I was employed by the studio. Judy was full of fears. I urged her to enjoy being the great star that she was but she didn't know how to do that.'[77] Filming *The Pirate* was a nightmare. Judy was smoking 80 cigarettes a day, not eating and being nauseous at the thought of eating which, for once, worried the studio heads. She was also, thanks to a 'friendly' studio masseuse, out of her head on pills during most of the filming, missing 99 of the 135-day schedule. The drugs caused paranoia, the paranoia was addressed to her husband and the film was a financial flop.

The one bright point during filming was Liza's christening at the Episcopal Church on Santa Monica Boulevard and Camden Drive in Beverly Hills, California. She even appeared in *The Pirate* sitting on her mother's lap. Judy told the press, 'This was just for fun and there'll be no more roles for Liza until she's able to pick them for herself.'[78] However, once the christening was over Judy felt herself flung into a terrible loneliness. Liza was mainly looked after by the nanny, a Miss (or Mrs) MacFarlane and Judy's psychiatrist Dr Simmel was ill.[79] He recommended other analysts for Judy but she was adamant that she did not want anyone else. It was all too, too much and the press could not be silenced forever. On 12 July 1947 the dam broke in the column of gossip writer Louella O Parsons. She wrote, 'Judy Garland is a very sick girl and has suffered a complete nervous collapse. For weeks there have been rumours that all was not well with Judy and Vincente Minnelli … Yesterday Minnelli said, "Judy is a very sick girl, and the only thing that is important now is to get her well. She is under a doctor's care and in a highly nervous state."'[80] Judy was taken to a private sanatorium in the Californian desert where she was treated for drug addiction, malnutrition and severe melancholia. It was just 16 months after she had given birth to Liza and a mere eight years after she had wowed the world in *The Wizard of Oz*.

It was a terrible experience for Judy. She was to later tell *McCall's*, 'About the second day I noticed that [the other patients] all used to gather on the lawn near my bungalow. I finally wandered our on the law one day and joined the group … As far as I could gather not one of them was demented in the common sense. Most of them were just too highly strung and too sensitive for reality … I realised that I had a great deal in common with them, in the sense that they had been concentrating on themselves too strongly, the same as I'.[81] At 5 a.m. every day Judy's room was searched for pills while she was supposed to be asleep. 'Every bottle, every drawer, every stitch of clothing, every corner. It took me five mornings to get up enough courage to ask her what she was looking for. The first time I asked her she didn't even answer me. She just kept looking'.[82]

Although it seemed like things could not get any worse, they did. The sanatorium cost Judy $300 a day. The studio suspended her which meant that she would not be paid until she returned to work. And finally, the government announced that Ethel had not paid all the taxes she should have on Judy's earnings and placed a lien on them. Minnelli, busy on a film, had initially refused to take Liza to see her mother but finally he relented. Again Judy to *McCall's*, 'She toddled into my bungalow and into my arms. I didn't know what to say to her. She wasn't 2-years-old. I just held her, and she kept kissing me and looking at me with those huge, helpless brown eyes of hers. I jabbered a little but mostly held her. But we laughed, too. After a short while they took her away. I lay down on the bed and started to cry. There have been many blue moments in my life, but I never remember having such a feeling.'[83]

As Judy and Minnelli approached their second wedding anniversary, the strain was beginning to tell. For a second time her husband was siding against her and with the studio. They lived a life befitting an international movie star and her film director husband. Unfortunately, they did not have the financial wherewithal to meet the costs that such a lifestyle demanded. Ethel had wrecked Judy's financial security and Minnelli, although he earned a good salary, had not been a heavy earner for long enough to have accrued any savings to offset unexpected bills (such as Judy's hospitalisation) or demands for back taxes. Judy sought solace in an affair with Yul Brynner and then caught Minnelli in bed with the handyman. It was now that Judy suffered what would be reported in the press as 'another phony suicide attempt'. Unable to sleep properly for 13 days and nights she took far too many sleeping pills but was found before she could suffer any lasting damage. Judy also found herself a younger, more attractive psychiatrist in the form of Dr Herbert Kupper.

While Judy was suffering, Minnelli was doting on Liza. He gave into her every whim: she wanted to go to the studio; Minnelli took her to the studio. She wanted to ride on the boom that raised and lowered the cameras, no problem. Much later Liza recalled, 'He really understood me. He treated me like such a lady. Even then he dealt with me on a feminine level. To do that to a little girl is probably the most valuable thing that can happen.'[84]

Dr Kupper believed that Judy needed institutionalised care and Judy was due to be admitted to the Austen Riggs Foundation[85] at Main Street, Stockbridge, Massachusetts on 4 August 1947. Judy would be under the care of Dr Edward Knight but he was not due to arrive in Massachusetts until 8 August. Judy convinced Dr Kupper that she could not be without help for any period of time, however short, so he accompanied her to Austen Riggs. It was a mistake. Another error came when Judy did not go straight to the centre but booked into the Red Lion Inn with Dr Kupper, a maid and a secretary. Whenever she left her room, fans wanting to say hello besieged Judy. It was intolerable for someone who did not like to be touched by strangers and she locked herself away in her room. Judy became reliant on Dr Kupper and when Dr Knight arrived on 8 August to begin treatment on the 15th he found himself undermined by Dr Kupper. The two men argued and Dr Knight threatened to refuse to treat Judy unless Dr Kupper absented himself. For a time the two analysts engaged in a stand-off before Dr Kupper blinked first and left for California on 14 August. Intense therapy began the next day. Judy's relationship with her father was laid bare. She revealed that she believed her father was homosexual and blamed this entirely on Ethel. She also told the analyst that when her father was taken to hospital, a fluid was seeping from his ear. He picked up a favourite blanket of Judy's to stem the flow. After his death Judy kept the blanket close to her but one day it went missing. Ethel had thrown it away and Judy never forgave her mother for this treachery. After each day's session Judy returned to the Red Lion exhausted but unable to sleep unless she swallowed a handful of pills. Dr Knight insisted that Judy move into the centre. At the Red Lion Judy had an element of freedom that would have been unavailable to her inside the centre. She was in constant telephone contact with Minnelli, Liza, Dr Kupper, her agent and manager. She was informed that she was to be cast in *The Barkeleys of Broadway* opposite Fred Astaire. Without informing Dr Knight or anyone else at the Austen Riggs Centre

Judy flew back to the West Coast. Charles Walters was to direct and since Judy had gained some weight while in Massachusetts she was put on a diet. Her old demons quickly returned and she began drinking when the pills didn't work. On 19 July MGM sacked her and replaced her with Ginger Rogers.

Around this time the first vestiges of the horror that would become known as 'McCarthyism' began to raise its ugly head in Hollywood and Washington. Many of Judy's friends were accused of having Communist sympathies. Judy despised the thought of witch-hunts and issued a statement that read, 'Before every free conscience in America is subpoenaed, please speak up! Say your piece. Write your congressman a letter! Let the Congress know what you think of its "Un-American Committee". Tell them how much you resent the way Mr Thomas[86] is kicking the living daylights out of the Bill of Rights.'[87] When he read the statement Louis B Mayer was incandescent with fury. He read Judy the riot act – he did not like his 'children' becoming involved in politics especially on the opposite side to him.

The ever-present studio decided that Judy and Gene Kelly could become an adult version of the teen Judy and Mickey Rooney. What was worse from Judy's point of view was that Minnelli was in full agreement with their idea. Finally, Judy stood her ground – she refused to work with her husband. She even had him replaced on *Easter Parade* (1948), her next picture, much to his disappointment and embarrassment.

Charles 'Chuck' Walters was lined up to direct Judy and Gene Kelly in the film. Judy was looking forward to working with Kelly again. It was not to be – playing volleyball on 12 October two days before filming was due to start, he broke his ankle and four days later was replaced by Fred Astaire who had not made a film in two years and had to be coaxed out of 'retirement'.

A scene from the film 'Easter Parade.' Judy and Fred Astaire do a comic dance dressed as a pair of hoboes. 1947

Fred Astaire (10 May 1899–22 June 1987) was born on South 10th Street in Omaha, Nebraska, as Frederic Austerlitz, Jr. In January 1933 5ft 9in Astaire was given a screen test by RKO, It wasn't good: 'Can't act. Slightly bald. Also dances.' His first major rôle was playing himself in MGM's *Dancing Lady* (1933). It was the next film, *Flying Down To Rio* (1933) for RKO, co-starring Dolores Del Rio, Gene Raymond and Ginger Rogers that established him as a star. Astaire spent hours on set practising his steps. 'Choreography for the camera requires 80 per cent brain work and 20 per cent footwork,' he once remarked. He appeared together with Ginger Rogers in ten films. In 1949 he was awarded a special Oscar in recognition of his contribution to film. Astaire died of pneumonia aged 88 in Century City Hospital, Los Angeles.

Easter Parade, which was filmed between 25 November 1947 and 9 February 1948, had an excellent score written by Irving Berlin that featured such hit numbers as *A Couple of Swells*, *Better Luck Next Time* and *When the Midnight Choo-Choo Leaves for Alabama*. Judy received top billing and she gave one of her best performances as Hannah Brown, the chorus girl that Don Hewes (Astaire) bets that he can make into a leading lady replacing Nadine Hale (Ann Miller).[88] Judy was determined to put on a brave face for her daughter, her public and her now uninterested husband. The Internal Revenue Service took most of her salary for *Easter Parade*. Her next job was a bit part playing herself in Norman Taurog's all-star *Words and Music*. Judy sang *Johnny One-Note* and with Mickey Rooney, gloriously miscast as the gay lyricist Lorenz Hart, she performed *I Wish I Were In Love Again*. *Words and Music* would be the last time that the pair appeared on celluloid together. Rooney was nearly 30, on his third marriage and feared the end of his career. He was finding work difficult to come by, so inextricably linked was he with the Andy Hardy persona. Filming was not a happy experience for either of them. Judy was now suffering from cripplingly painful migraines and Minnelli was of little help, believing most of his wife's illnesses to be psychosomatic. He was embarrassed by her and, as a consequence, mostly left her to her own devices. MGM promised Judy a paid six-month break if she appeared in *Words and Music*. As she downed yet more pills, she clung to the thought of the rest and relaxation she would enjoy during her half-year off.

In the summer of 1948 Judy's drug addiction had become public knowledge to anyone who read the scandal sheet *Hollywood Nite Life*. The publication devoted three front-page stories to the story of a celebrated Hollywood star's battle with drugs. The star was a 'pill-head' and to anyone who didn't know the identity of the person in question the journalists on the title helpfully referred to her as 'Miss G'.[89]

Then MGM decided not to give Judy the time off and ordered her back to the studio to play Annie Oakley in *Annie Get Your Gun*, Irving Berlin's smash-hit musical. Judy accepted the role but then was shocked to discover that her hair was falling out in clumps because of the drugs she was taking. The first task MGM put before her was to learn how to shoot; then came vocal coaching to get the correct accent. Judy went into the recording studio to lay down the tracks that would be used when she sang on film. The recordings were terrific and are now collectors' items. Her co-star Howard Keel broke his leg thanks to the foolishness of director Busby Berkeley. Keel was to gently ride a horse across the soundstage. Berkeley had other ideas and insisted the horse gallop. It did and slipped on the shiny floor and fell on top of Keel, breaking his leg. The focus of the shooting fell on Judy and she was not that good and she knew it. Judy looked tired and thin and more importantly (for the studio) she was giving a bad performance. On 3 May 1949 Berkeley was sacked and replaced by Chuck Walters. He was appalled by what was in the can and decided that none of it could be saved. A week later, on 10 May 1949, while she was rehearsing the *I'm An Indian Too* number, Judy was summarily sacked by messenger. Betty Hutton replaced her, ten days later, on 20 May 1949.

Back at home Minnelli was of no use. Judy locked herself in her room and contemplated suicide. Her career was over. Her second marriage was over in all but name. The press had taken against her. Then Joe Pasternak called with an offer of work. His leading lady June Allyson was pregnant and Pasternak needed to replace her on *In the Good Old Summertime* (1949). Judy had been put on suspension after being sacked from *Annie Get Your*

Gun and the front office was against Pasternak's hiring of Judy. He persisted and finally they relented. Little did he know it, but he had just saved Judy's life. It meant no break and Judy had to report for work immediately. *In the Good Old Summertime* was a musical remake of *The Shop Around The Corner* (1940)[90] which had starred Jimmy Stewart, Margaret Sullavan and Frank Morgan. Rather than force Judy to go on yet another crash diet, Pasternak covered her weight gain by clever use of costume. Judy's co-stars were Van Johnson, Buster Keaton, Spring Byinton and S Z Sakall, known to all as 'Cuddles'.

On 31 March 1949, not long after the completion of *In the Good Old Summertime*, Judy and Minnelli announced their marriage was at an end. Without the heartache that Judy brought him Minnelli seemed to thrive and his career flourished as he directed highly successful musicals for MGM.

For Judy all her demons once again came flooding back and she realised that she needed professional help. On 29 May 1949 with her new manager Carleton Alsop in tow Judy admitted herself to the Peter Bent Brigham Hospital in Boston, Massachusetts. Louis B Mayer met Judy's hospital bills for the 13-week stay, as she was broke. It was there that she went 'cold turkey' – drugs and alcohol were withdrawn from her quickly. Lights went off at 9 p.m. whether she was asleep or not and she was given three hearty meals a day. The hospital had a wing for retarded children and as part of her treatment, it was decided that Judy should spend an hour a day entertaining these children.[91] Judy was at first uncertain but she was recognised by the children who had seen her in *The Wizard of Oz*. Judy was soon spending much of the time with one girl not much older than Liza. This girl, who hadn't once spoken in the two years she had been in the institution, had been abandoned by her family and received no visitors.

Judy chatted to her about anything and everything, not expecting any response. When the 13 weeks were up Mayer insisted that Judy return to the studio or be released from her contract which would allow the company to stop paying the bills. Joe Pasternak offered her a role in his new film *Summer Stock* and Judy gratefully accepted. The staff at the Peter Bent Brigham Hospital were horrified and insisted that Judy should stay for another three months to fully recover. Judy ignored their advice and discharged herself. Before she left she went to say goodbye to her young friends in the mental ward and sought out the silent girl. At first she ignored Judy then screamed her name at the top of her voice and wrapped her tiny arms around Judy. She shouted, 'I love you, I love you'. Carleton Alsop tapped Judy and motioned for her to leave saying that they would miss the train, Judy replied, 'We'll just have to miss the train. I'm not going to leave this child while she's talking'[92] and Judy stayed in the ward for several hours until the child fell into a fitful sleep. Judy later said, 'I guess it was one of the great moments of my life when that child spoke like that. I just didn't give a damn how many pictures I'd been fired from, or how much humiliation … I had done a human being some good. I felt on top of the world.'[93]

When Judy returned to MGM she was 15lb heavier than when she had left. Almost inevitably the note came down from the front office, 'Lose 15lb'. Judy went back to her pill diet but only lost 7lb in 11 days. Incredibly, gossip columnist Louella O Parsons wrote on her column, 'I could spank Judy for not doing what the studio asks.' Pasternak did not mind and allowed Judy to play the role of farm girl Jane Falbury at the weight she was. The story concerned Jane who owned a farm in New England and allowed a repertory company (stock company in America) to use her barn and then fell in love with the star of the show. Despite Pasternak's

Judy and friends, Jean Simmons and Laurence Harvey, at a party in Beverly Hills in 1950

benign interest, it was not a happy company. Judy was back on the pills and this caused her behaviour to be, to say the least, erratic. She was late most days, refused to shoot retakes, wouldn't rehearse and lost her temper with almost everyone. Both director Charles Walters and co-star Gene Kelly refused to work with her again.

A fortnight after shooting ended the studio decided that it needed another song-and-dance number to balance out the film.

Judy was recalled to shoot the song *Get Happy* and the cast and crew were shocked by her appearance. She had lost almost a stone and a half and she looked ill. The studio now faced a dilemma – did it shoot anyway and hope that the audiences didn't notice that in that one scene of the film Judy was two stone lighter than in the rest of the movie. It was decided to proceed and shoot anyway. Every critic picked up on the glaring difference but that scene was the best part of the picture so they virtually glossed over it. After shooting finally wrapped Judy was sent with Liza to Carmel, a seaside resort in California, for some much needed rest and recuperation.[94] Usually, studio flacks would do their best to keep the bad behaviour of their stars out of the press but with Judy that was all but impossible. Other celebrities even began commenting on her. Joan Crawford said, 'I didn't know her well, but after watching her in action I didn't want to know her well.'[95]

Judy was supposed to spend six months in Carmel but after just three weeks the studio came a-calling and told Judy that she was to replace the pregnant June Allyson in *Royal Wedding* (1951), which would co-star Fred Astaire and was written by Alan Jay Lerner. The film was set around the wedding of Princess Elizabeth to Prince Philip of Greece in November 1947. It was an amazing decision since the lead female would participate in seven musical numbers. Mayer, it seemed, had not learned any lessons from the fiasco that was Judy's casting in *Annie Get Your Gun*. Perhaps he believed that Judy's illness was not as serious as she led everyone to believe. He even went so far as to call her 'a spoiled, bad girl having a temper tantrum'[96] in one interview he gave. But if Mayer was not aware of the seriousness of Judy's condition, it appeared that nor was the lady herself. Judy quickly agreed to make *Royal Wedding*. Judy was aware of the poor press she was receiving and may have believed that the gentlemen of the Fourth

Estate might give her an easier time if they saw that MGM had restored its faith in her.

Judy flung herself into rehearsals and costume fittings on 16 June 1950 and also back into the nightmare of pills. She was sacked the next day. The press had a field day, insinuating none too subtly that Judy was a drug addict and an alcoholic. On 19 June 1950, distraught, she rang Minnelli and Carleton Alsop and both arrived at her home within minutes. Neither dissuaded Judy from reading the terrible baiting she was receiving in the press and she lay in her bed reading the newspapers. Both men were downstairs discussing the situation while Liza slept in her bedroom. Judy walked slowly into her bathroom and locked the door. She smashed a tumbler and, with a jagged piece, she cut her own throat. As soon as she saw blood spurt from the wound she unlocked the door, ran back to her bed and screamed hysterically. Minnelli and Alsop were by her side in seconds wondering what the noise was about. They took her to a friend's house where a doctor was summoned, only to find that the damage was superficial. Alsop was to comment that he had suffered more serious wounds shaving.[97] Two days later, UP reported that MGM had announced that Judy would probably not be making any more films for the studio and that Jane Powell was auditioning for the female lead in *Royal Wedding*. It was all over for Judy at MGM. The studio for whom Judy had made 28 films in 16 years that had grossed more than $80,000,000 at the box office summarily washed its hands of her on 29 September 1950. There would be no pay off, no pension fund, no farewell party. Louis B Mayer announced rather disingenuously, "I couldn't have done more for her had she been my own daughter."[98]

With a house to pay for and no income, Judy asked Mayer for a loan. He telephoned Nicholas Schenck, the chairman of

Loew's Inc but he refused. Mayer offered Judy a personal loan and she accepted. Judy left Mayer's office and the MGM lot, broke, unemployed and with a very uncertain future.

Judy wrote an open letter to her fans which was published in *Modern Screen* in November 1950. It read:

'Dear Friends,
This is a thank-you note.

At a time when I've been gossip's victim and the target of a thousand lies, you people have stood by me. I won't ever forget that.

You've judged me not on the basis of headlines, rumour and innuendo but on my performances as an actress and entertainer.

Ever since the release of my last picture, *Summer Stock*, thousands of you have had the kindness to write me. You've congratulated me, encouraged me, and pledged me your support. And for all this – let me repeat – I'm eternally grateful. Inasmuch as it is impossible for me to reply individually to your more than 18,000 letters, I'm using this space in *Modern Screen* to answer those questions most frequently asked.

I have a responsibility to you friends. Rather than let you be misguided by the flood of nonsense printed about me by reporters and uninformed writers who know none of the facts, I intend to fulfil my responsibility by telling you moviegoers the truth.

I am not quitting motion pictures. Movies are my life's blood. I love making motion pictures and always have ever since I was a little girl.

I do not intend, however, to make any films for the next six months. I'm just going to relax, take things easy, and regain my peace of mind.

For a while I expected to go to Paris with my daughter, Liza, and my husband, Vincente Minnelli – but his studio has decided to film all of *An American in Paris* in Hollywood, and since he is directing that picture and plans shortly to direct the sequel to *Father of the Bride*, we all plan to remain in California.

I love to work, I love to sing, I love to act – I get restless when I don't – and it's entirely possible that I will do a few broadcasts with Bing Crosby or Bob Hope before six months are up.

My health is fine. As I write this, I've just returned from a vacation in Sun Valley and Lake Tahoe. I'm sun-tanned, I weigh 110 pounds, and my outlook on things is joyful and optimistic.

Many of you have written and asked what was wrong with me in the past.

The honest answer is that I suffered from a mild sort of inferiority complex. I used to work myself up into depressions, thought no one really cared about me, no one outside my family, that is.

Why I should have ever gotten depressed, I certainly don't know. You people have proved to me that I've got thousands of friends the world over, that you care about my welfare and my career.

It's perfectly normal for people to have their ups and downs. I know that now, but a year or so ago, these depressions of mine used to worry me, and the more I worried about them, the lower I felt.

Anyway, all of that is gone and done with. The slate of the past is wiped clean. Insofar as I'm concerned, the world is good, golden and glorious. My best years and my best work lie ahead of me, and I'm going to give them everything I've got.

Many of you have asked if I realised how closely you followed my career and behaviour. I certainly do, and that's why I want all of you to know, especially the youngsters, that I'm not in the slightest embittered about Hollywood and that I still think a motion picture career is one of the finest ambitions any girl can have.

It means hard work and it has its pitfalls but so has every other occupation.

If my daughter, Liza, wants to become an actress, I'll do everything to help her.

Of course, being a child actress and being raised on a studio lot is not the easiest adjustment a young girl can make. You don't go to baseball games or junior proms or sorority initiations, but every success has its sacrifices, and these are the ones a very young girl must make if she wants a career at a very early age.

The girl who finishes her schooling, however, and then wants to become an actress is facing a thrilling, rewarding career.

If I had to do it all over again, I would probably make the same choices and the same errors. These are part of living.

A lot of fanciful stories have depicted me as the victim of stark tragedy, high drama, and all sorts of mysterious Hollywood meanderings. All that is bunk.

Basically, I am still Judy Garland, a plain American girl from Grand Rapids, Minnesota, who's had a lot of good breaks, a few tough breaks, and who loves you with all her heart for your kindness in understanding that I am nothing more, nothing less.

Thank you again.
Judy Garland'[99]

Chapter 6

Strike Up the Band

Judy's final film with MGM, *Summer Stock*, had yet to be released and Judy knew that she had given a good performance but she also knew that that would not be enough to rescue her professional life. There was nowhere for her to go: MGM did not want her back and Twentieth Century-Fox were grooming a starlet by the name of Marilyn Monroe who had shown promise in *The Asphalt Jungle* (1950) and *All About Eve* (1950). Even if another studio had been willing to take the risk of hiring Judy, her name had been blackened by MGM so no one would give her a job. Judy had become a pariah in the city that made her a star. She was also completely incapable of acting in the way that normal people did when they lost a job. For Judy there could be no such thing as an economy drive – she was a star and that was the way she had to live.

Judy moved into the Beverly Hills Hotel and into a suite that cost her more than $150 a day. She had no real concept of money or its worth because her financial needs had been looked after (or not, as the case might be) by her mother and stepfather or manager or accountants. Judy was also now without an agent as her previous representatives, Phil Berg and Burt Allenberg, had dissolved their firm the Berg-Allenberg Agency after they split up their partnership.

Then salvation came in a most unlikely form. Ethel arrived to save the day (and career) for her youngest daughter.[100] Ethel's solution was to return Judy to her show-business roots and put her back on the live stage. It had been some time since Ethel had been getting work for her daughter and so many of her contacts were out of date. In the end she approached the Cal-Neva Lodge on Lake Tahoe and booked Judy in there. Then mother and daughter approached Roger Edens and asked him to work out an act for Judy. Judy spent several weeks at the Cal-Neva Lodge with Roger Edens rehearsing her new act and then for reasons that remain unknown she suddenly left and returned to the Beverly Hills Hotel where, ensconced in her room, she went on an eating binge and put on more than two stones. Then she upped sticks and after sending Liza to live with Minnelli she moved to New York where she booked herself into a luxury hotel. She wandered the streets, watched the 1950 World Series, chatted with her fans and got even fatter.

At a cocktail party hosted by Jackie Gleason, Judy once again met Sidney Luft, a former test pilot who had been married to the lesbian actress Lynn Bari, known as the 'Queen of the GIs'. However, Luft ignored Judy at first. However, they began dating when Judy found she could talk easily to him. She was to later claim that it was love at first sight. When Judy returned to Los Angeles, Luft followed her He suggested that he became her manager although Judy demurred and in October 1950 she signed with the William Morris Agency.

Michael Sidney Luft (2 November 1915–15 September 2005) hailed from a small, middle-class Jewish family and was born in New Rochelle and grew up in Bronxville, New York. He was educated at the Hun School in Princeton before attending university in Pennsylvania and Miami. In 1934 he married but divorced within a year. He joined the Royal Canadian Air Force in 1940 (some records say 1941) and later became a test pilot for Douglas and worked on a few films in minor roles. Luft was a heavy drinker, big-time gambler and bar room brawler. For a time he worked as secretary to the dancer Eleanor Powell and by all accounts also provided a more intimate service. For eight years he managed the career of his second wife Lynn Bari whom he married on 28 November 1943 and by whom she had a son, John Michael, in 1948. The couple was divorced on Boxing Day 1950 with Bari citing cruelty, complaining that Luft took too long to buy his evening newspaper. He left her at 6 p.m. and did not return until the early hours, explaining he had been 'out with the boys'. She also complained that she had loaned him $16,000 in cash and her $13,000 equity in property to invest in a film, but that 'he threatened to sell or mortgage the properties in order to deprive her and their child of a share in the proceeds'. She did not have the charisma to be a big star and Luft often found himself frustrated. He worked briefly as a talent agent and produced two B-movies for the Monogram studio, *Kilroy Was Here* (1947) and the sequel, *French Leave* (1948), both featuring the former child stars Jackie Cooper and Jackie Coogan.

Judy appeared on eight radio shows with Bing Crosby and recorded an album. She had just enough work to keep herself and Luft who by now was acting as her business manager. On 21 December 1950 the Minnellis announced that their marriage was over. Judy divorced Minnelli on 23 March 1951 claiming mental cruelty and adding that Minnelli often left her alone. The judge ruled that although Judy was to have custody of Liza, the five-year-old should spend six months of the year with her father.

If Judy and Luft were to become an item the Hollywood press did not rate their chances of a happy union. The magazine *Modern Screen* reported in May 1951, 'Sid Luft, better known to nightclubbers as "One-Punch Luft" because he's handy with his fists, is one of those personable young men who's been around Hollywood for years … Everyone in Hollywood wishes Judy happiness. She, more than any other person, deserves a break in her personal life. Yet, somehow, the feeling circulates that if and when she becomes Luft's wife, she will be embarking on a marriage that cannot possibly last.'[101]

On Monday 9 April 1951 Judy opened at the London Palladium in a show that would revitalise her career. However, when Judy disembarked from the liner *Ile de France* both fans and press were surprised at her appearance. Although Judy was 28 she looked as if she was in her mid-40s and she was fat, weighing more than 10 stone. Her hair was thinning and dyed jet black. Nevertheless the press gave her a warm welcome but not as warm as that afforded by a London that was still in the throes of wartime rationing. In her dressing room before the curtain went up Judy was a bundle of nerves unable to sit, eat or even stand still – constantly walking up and down. As she walked on stage she received an incredible ovation and she blew the audience kisses in response telling them, 'This is the greatest moment of my life.'[102] When she joked about her weight, they screamed 'There's more to love!' She took her shoes off and walked around the stage in her stockinged feet keeping time with her big toe. The crowd lapped it up. At the end she sat on the edge of the stage in pitch blackness apart from one spotlight shining on her and sang *Somewhere Over the Rainbow*. As she took an ovation, she got up, put her shoes back on and then tripped over a microphone lead and fell over. She left the stage but returned for an encore. Despite her nerves Judy gave

a bravura performance egged on by an audience that loved her. The press also loved her, with *The Times* reporting, 'Miss Judy Garland not only tops the bill at the Palladium this week, she also runs away with the show.'[103] The reviews were unanimously good although they did gently mock her choice of outfits. Judy became the toast of London – celebrities came backstage after each performance to chat and to congratulate her. After four weeks in London Judy began touring Britain opening at the Glasgow Empire on 21 May, the Edinburgh Empire on 29 May and, after spending her 29th birthday in Paris, opened in Manchester on 11 June 1951. The tour finished in July in the unglamorous setting of Birmingham but Judy was elated and so were her many fans.

The Palace Theatre in New York's Duffy Square at 1564 Broadway had always held an almost mystic appeal for Judy. In a dozen or so of her films her character's aim was to appear at the Palace and sometimes she made it and sometimes she did not. Judy Garland had never played the Palace and now with the success of her European tour, especially the London leg, Judy wanted more than ever to appear at the venerated venue. Like many theatres, the Palace found it difficult to keep up with the growing changes in entertainment and began showing films rather than straight variety until eventually it succumbed to the inevitable and became a cinema. However, in 1949, the year that *In the Good Old Summertime* was released, the Palace Theatre resumed its variety fare combining it with the latest cinematic releases. On 16 October 1951 Judy opened at the Palace, performing twice daily. That month was a terrific one for live theatre: Gertrude Lawrence was wowing audiences on Broadway playing opposite Yul Brynner in Rodgers & Hammerstein's smash hit musical *The King and I* while Katharine Hepburn was appearing in Shakespeare's *As You Like It*. But it was Judy at the Palace that was really setting New

Judy's debut at the London Palladium was a popular and critical sensation. She acknowledges the applause in Cornell Capa's 1951 photograph

York theatre land alight. Tickets cost $6 and the show was a sell-out. Backstage before the show, Judy was suffering from nerves – she was as concerned that the celebrities in the audience would be shocked by her weight as worried by her performance. She had lost weight since her London shows six months earlier, but she was still overweight and looked nothing like the cinematic version of herself. The audience included such luminaries as Jack Benny, Marlene Dietrich, Jimmy Durante, Gloria Swanson and the Duke and Duchess of Windsor, the former King Edward VIII and Mrs Simpson. Judy was due to appear as the first act in the second half, the opening half of the show having been closed by the English comedian Max Bygraves.

After the interval the red curtains opened to reveal eight handsome chorus boys listed in the programme as 'Judy's Eight Boy Friends'. As they parted Judy was revealed wearing a black velvet gown. The crowd went wild – Judy was home. She sang a number of songs made famous by previous Palace habitués and then launched into renditions of her own material – *You Made Me Love You*, *The Trolley Song*, *Rock-a-Bye Your Baby* and many more. After the Boy Friends had done a routine Judy returned clad in black tights, top hat and a tuxedo jacket and sang *Get Happy* from *Summer Stock*. Another quick change and Judy appeared in a tramp's costume and, with a male partner, sang the number *We're A Couple of Swells* from *Easter Parade*. The audience again roared its approval and Judy waited, stock-still on stage, until they became quiet. When silence finally reigned in the theatre Judy took her battered top hat and walked to the footlights where in a lone spotlight she sang her signature theme *Somewhere Over the Rainbow*. A three-minute ovation ensued. A celebratory party was held at the 21 Club following the triumphant performance. By a strange coincidence the

New York Journal-American's reviewer for the show was none other than Robert Garland, the man whose surname Judy had adopted all those years earlier. Judy's itinerary was relentless and it affected her health. On a Sunday less than a month after the opening, she collapsed and was taken to the Le Roy Hospital on 61st Street where she was treated for nervous exhaustion. By the following Wednesday she was back on stage and for 15 more weeks Judy performed finally closing on Sunday 24 February 1952, having performed before an astonishing 800,000 people. Judy was paid $20,000 a week to appear at the Palace, a not untidy sum of $380,000. The money was entrusted to Sid Luft and Abe Lastfogel of the William Morris Agency to manage on Judy's behalf.

Sid Luft managed every aspect of Judy's life and she was madly in love with him – she felt protected, secure, worshipped and respected but, at the back of her mind, her basic insecurities still nagged at her. He said, 'I love Judy. I want to protect her from the trauma she once knew. I don't want her to be bewildered or hurt again. I want her to have happiness. Neither I, nor anyone else, can ever force her to do anything she doesn't want to do.'[104]

'I grew up in a rough New York neighbourhood,' he said, 'and didn't put up with shit from anyone. I'm a survivor, with the scars to show for it, and I think that appealed to Judy. She needed someone to lean on who wouldn't crack.'[105] Judy loved the fact that Luft took control but there was still that feeling … It may have been her certainty that Luft wanted what she wanted and would help and manage her career that made Judy unconcerned about where all the money she was earning was going. Many years later after she and Luft split, Judy was to claim that she had never seen a single cent of the money that she had earned.

Jack Warner, writing in his autobiography, said of Luft 'He's one of the original guys who promised his parents he'd never work a day in his life and made good' but Lauren Bacall, a friend of Judy and her husband, later defended Luft: 'Sid was a wheeler-dealer, but not a bad guy. He and Judy were crazy about each other … He gave her a semblance of family life. And he always took care of his children, he was devoted to them … Judy had a hard time dealing with life, she needed constant reassurance. Whatever quirks Sid may have had, he was the one who helped her get through.'

Meantime, Judy and Luft flew to Los Angeles where she was to open at the Philharmonic Auditorium on 21 April. It was in the City of the Angels that Luft and Ethel first met and they took an instant dislike to each other. Ethel quickly realised how much Judy depended on Luft and that if a choice had to be made between them her daughter would surely choose her man over her mother. Ethel unwisely gave an interview to the press in which he was less than complimentary about her daughter's boyfriend.

Judy had once again acquired star status thanks to her performances at the Palace in New York and so everyone on the West Coast now wanted to see her. Tickets were snapped up by touts and were offered at the exorbitant rate of $100 per pair. Many paid up and they were treated to a show every bit as successful as the ones at the Palladium and the Palace. The four-week run was a sell-out. Decca released a live recording of the New York show, *Judy at the Palace*, and Judy signed a five-year deal with RCA Victor Records. While in California she received news that her divorce from Vincente Minnelli had become final.

On 1 October 1951 Judy and Luft were driving home after dinner out when he ignored a red light at La Cienega and Beverley Boulevards and hit another car which careered into a third.

Judy got into an argument with a passenger in one of the other cars and hit him. A passing dentist stopped to help and Sid belted him as well. At 3.15 a.m. Sid was charged with four offences including drunk driving and thrown into jail. The drunk-driving charge was the only one that stuck and Sid was fined $150.[106]

On 8 June 1952 at 6 p.m. at the Hollister, California ranch of Robert Law, a friend of the couple, Judy and Luft were married. The ceremony lasted just five minutes. Judy spent her wedding night, two days before her 30th birthday, performing in her show at the Curran Theatre in San Francisco. Judy was also four months pregnant. 'She had a very sensuous body,' recalled Luft in 2001. 'Up close, her skin was like porcelain, pure white. I was crazy about her.'[107] Within hours of the ceremony the previous Mrs Sid Luft, Lynn Bari, sued her ex-husband for support in child maintenance. Bari claimed that the monthly sum of $200 paid by Luft was insufficient to meet the needs of their son John and demanded $500. Sitting in the Superior Court in Hollywood, Judge Burke agreed to a raise but only to $400. As if one court case was not enough to shatter the newlyweds' happiness, Ethel also decided it was her turn to have her day in court and sued Judy for non-support. For once Judy stood up to her mother and showed the court the money that Ethel had received. She also pointed out that her mother was a talented singing and music teacher who was quite capable of earning her own living. The case was dismissed but it created a wider rift between mother and daughter.

Hell hath no fury like a mother who loses a court case and Ethel bleated her moans to the one-legged gossip columnist Sheilah Graham on 19 July 1952. 'Judy has been selfish all her life,' said Ethel, conveniently rewriting history. 'That's my fault. I made it too easy for her. She's worked, but that's all she ever

Judy and Sid Luft travelled to New York with Liza to attend the premiere of 'A Star is Born' in 1954

wanted, to be an actress. She never said, "I want to be kind or loved" only "I want to be famous".'[108] Ethel then asked that the media should forget her, as Judy had obviously done. And just to make sure that she was forgotten when she landed a $61-a-week job[109] working on the assembly line for Douglas Aircraft, she immediately told the press.

Judy's second pregnancy was not a particularly happy one, especially in the last trimester. Already overweight, she suffered from dropsy which made her obese and although Sid Luft was apparently conscientious when it came to arranging Judy's career, he was less than attentive when it came to being a husband. Judy recalled, 'From the beginning Sid and I weren't happy. I don't know why. I really don't. For me it was work, work, work; and then I didn't see much of Sid. He was always dashing off to places lining up my appearances. I wasn't made any happier looking into mirrors seeing myself balloon out of shape from liquids trapped in my body.'[110]

Judy's second daughter was born on 21 November 1952 and christened Lorna. There are a number of reasons for the name. Judy liked it because it was the female lead in Clifford Odets's *Golden Boy*. Sid named Lorna after his mother Leonora and because when he was much younger he had been keen on a girl named Lorna Doone.[111] Six weeks later as one female member of the Garland family was enjoying her new life, another died. At 7.30 a.m. on 5 January 1953 Ethel dropped dead from a heart seizure in the car park of Douglas Aircraft. She was discovered four hours later between two cars as she had desperately tried to get help. She was 59 years old.[112]

When she heard the news Judy collapsed and when the press got wind of Ethel's death they rehashed all the tales of how mean Judy had been to her mother and how Ethel had only ever wanted the best for her youngest daughter. Judy was advised by doctors not to go to her mother's funeral but she ignored them. Supported by Sid Luft and another friend, she managed to get through the ordeal on 8 January without collapsing. As soon as she was back home, however, Judy took to her bed, suffering mental anguish that was to last for two years and would wreck any chance the Lufts had of having a happy and successful marriage.

After what he regarded as a suitable period of mourning, Luft began to pressurise Judy into working. He felt that, having proved her talent on the stage, it was time for her to go back to movies. Luft also saw himself as a film producer so was now hoping to replicate Judy's stage success and previous cinematic triumphs a second time around.

Luft began to search for a suitable project for Judy. In December 1942 she had appeared in a radio production of *A Star is Born* for CBS's Lux Radio Theatre playing opposite Adolphe Menjou and Walter Pidgeon. At the time it had been suggested that she appear in a film version but MGM was distinctly cool on the idea. It felt that it would be wrong for the image that they had so meticulously arranged for Judy. Now more than ten years later, Judy was a free agent and she believed that *A Star is Born* would be perfect material for her cinematic return. Luft agreed but added that the film should be a musical. To get the project off the ground, Judy and Luft formed a production company, Transcona Enterprises.

The original version of *A Star is Born* premièred in Los Angeles on 20 April 1937. Directed by William Wellman, the film told the story of Esther Blodgett (Janet Gaynor), a wannabe film star who lands a job as a waitress at a Hollywood party where she meets the alcoholic actor Norman Maine (Fredric March). Through him she lands a screen test and is signed to a studio. She is given a new name, Vicki Lester. However, she quickly discovers that life in Tinseltown is not all glitz and glamour and even marriage to her screen idol does not make her happy. His career wanes as hers rises. She decides to give up her career to help look after him but when he hears this, he commits the supreme self-sacrifice by drowning himself, thus allowing Vicki to concentrate on her career. The character of Norman Maine was apparently based on several real actors, including John Barrymore, John Gilbert and John Bowers.[113] The film won an Oscar for Wellman and Robert Carson for Best Script from an Original Story. It was also nominated for Best Film (David O Selznick), Best Actor (March), Best Actress (Gaynor), Best Director (Wellman), Best Assistant Director (Eric Stacey), and Best Screenplay (Alan Campbell, Robert Carson, Dorothy Parker) plus an honorary award for W Howard Greene for colour photography.[114]

Legend has is that Sid Luft had the idea to ask George Cukor to direct Judy in a new version. Cukor was already celebrated for being a 'woman's director' and had already worked successfully with Katharine Hepburn in *A Bill of Divorcement* (1932), *Little Women* (1933), *Sylvia Scarlet* (1935), *The Philadelphia Story* (1940) and *Pat and Mike* (1952) which teamed her with long-term 'lover' Spencer Tracy; Joan Crawford in *No More Ladies* (1935), *The Women* (1939), *Susan and God* (1940) and *A Woman's Face* (1941); Greta Garbo in *Camille* (1936) and *Two-Faced Woman* (1941); Norma Shearer in *Romeo & Juliet* (1936), *The Women* (1939) and *Her Cardboard Lover* (1942); Ingrid Bergman in *Gaslight* (1944); Judy Holliday in *Winged Victory* (1944), *Adam's Rib* (1949), *Born Yesterday* (1950), *The Marrying Kind* (1952) and *It Should Happen to You* (1954) and Jean Simmons in *The Actress* (1953). However, at that time he had never directed a musical and was chary of accepting the job. He was impressed, however, by Moss Hart's script and he obviously knew the subject matter – actors and acting. It was his 37th film, his first musical, and his first full colour production.

Judy had been away from show business for far too long recovering from the mental anguish she suffered over Ethel's lonely death. It had been almost four years since she had stepped before a film camera and once again the press were referring to Judy as a has-been and, worse, suggested that the reason that she was overweight was not due to dropsy but because she was a hopeless alcoholic, and her management team dare not risk allowing her out in public in case she made a drunken show of herself. Judy's public image could not have been much worse. She had read the script and recognised many of her own failings in the character of Norman Maine and believed that if she played the role it would allow the public to see what she had been through – what she was going through.

Casting began in earnest and Cary Grant was lined up to play Norman Maine. Fortunately he pulled out before filming began, as the public would never have accepted the suave, tanned, healthy-looking Grant as an alcoholic has-been. Other names in the frame for the role are said to have included Humphrey Bogart, Gary Cooper, Marlon Brando and Montgomery Clift before James Mason stepped into the role. Judy was assigned the dressing room on the Warners' lot that had belonged to Bette Davis and on Monday 12 October Judy made her first appearance before a movie camera in more than three years. Luft presented Judy with a bracelet engraved 'Columbus discovered America on October 12, 1492. Judy Garland began principal photography on *A Star Is Born* on October 12, 1953. With all my love – Sid'.[115] With a budget estimated at $5,019,770 filming continued until 29 July 1954. More often than not, Judy had been playing herself,

George Cukor (7 July 1899–23 January 1983) was born in New York and began directing on Broadway in the 1920s before moving west in February 1929 to work as a dialogue director on *River Of Romance* (1929) and *All Quiet on the Western Front* (1930). Cukor's first directing rôle came in 1930 with *The Royal Family Of Broadway*. He began work on *Gone with the Wind* on 26 January 1939 but was sacked on 12 February after falling out with Clark Gable, a dismissal that rankled with him for the rest of his long life. Post-*A Star Is Born* (1954) he worked on *Lust For Life* (1956), *Bhowani Junction* (1956), *Let's Make Love* (1960), the unfinished *Something's Got to Give* (1962) and *My Fair Lady* (1964) which won him his only Oscar. His last film, made at the age of 82, was the disappointing *Rich And Famous* (1981).

or at least the MGM-manufactured self, or a simplistic part and playing Esther would be her first real acting challenge. It was a challenge that she met chemically as well as emotionally. Once again the spiral of uppers and downers and diet and sleeping pills began. It caused Judy to suffer extreme emotional highs and lows. Cukor was a tough taskmaster and then came the decision to reshoot everything shot in the first month. The footage had been filmed in WarnerScope (Warner Bros' own widescreen format) and WarnerColor before the decision was taken to use CinemaScope (which had to be licensed from Twentieth Century-Fox) and Technicolor. Judy was the only one to object to the idea but she was quickly overruled. Make-up artist Del Armstrong recalled, 'Cukor knew how to hurt a woman, and he used those tactics to get them into a mood for a crying scene.'[116] Luft had a very strange arrangement with Warner Bros – the entire negative cost of the film had to be recouped before he and Judy would be paid for their involvement. By the time filming wrapped the Lufts were deeply in debt. A number of key people had walked off the set and once again the press blamed Judy for this. It all became too much and she responded, 'I'm a little tired of being the patsy for the production delays on this film. It's easy to blame every production delay on the star. This was the story of my life at Metro when I was a child actress. When some problem came up and they couldn't lick the delay, no matter who caused it, it was always blamed on the star. Whoever was responsible figured that the star could get by without a bawling out. They couldn't.'[117]

By the end of the 10-month shoot Judy was once again a hopeless drug addict and she had fallen out of love with husband number three. Luft was bemused – all he had done, as far as he was concerned, was to help his wife get back to the top of the show-business tree.

Judy in a scene with James Mason in her triumphant return to the screen in the film, 'A Star is Born', 1954

95

Once again Judy's insecurity came rushing to the fore. 'Do you think we're all too close to it and we really don't have a good picture?' she asked Vern Alves, the film's assistant producer. 'But that can't be true. Of course, it's a good picture. Mason's great, the score is great, I'm great, the photography's great, it's a great picture … isn't it?'[118]

When the film premièred at the Pantages Theatre on 29 September 1954 Warner Bros' PR machine went into overdrive and described it as the 'Biggest Date in Entertainment History!' *The Hollywood Reporter* called it 'Hollywood's most eagerly anticipated film première in many years' and its reporter Mike Connolly said, 'Never have we seen people fight for seats as they did at this one … Were they rewarded? Yea verily. *Star* is an all-time great.' The film's opening was the first to be televised nationally and was such a ratings hit that it as rebroadcast the next night. Jack Warner said, 'It's the greatest night in the history of the movies.' Bosley Crowther, writing in *The New York Times*, opined, '[Cukor] gets performances from Miss Garland and Mr Mason that make the heart flutter and bleed.'[119] *A Star Is Born* premièred simultaneously in New York's Paramount and Victoria cinemas on 11 October and the reception it got was equally amazing. The audiences loved it and the press once again began writing favourably about Judy. Despite the hype the film did not live up to its pre-release expectations and was regarded as a box-office flop. True, Judy's financial situation was muddled to say the least. She still owed the government a fortune in unpaid taxes but she was nominated for an Oscar for her performance and discovered she was pregnant again.

On 29 March 1955 at the Cedars of Lebanon Hospital Judy gave birth to her third child, a son named Joseph Wiley, at 2 a.m. Frank Sinatra and Lauren Bacall kept Sid Luft company in the waiting room as he waited for the birth. The following night was the presentation of the 27th Academy Awards, broadcast from the RKO Pantages Theatre in Hollywood and the NBC Century Theatre in New York. The hosts were Bob Hope in Hollywood and Thelma Ritter in New York. The television show director Jean Negulesco (and also director of the Best Film nominated, *Three Coins in a Fountain*) said that he had been hoping that Judy's new baby would have been born during the broadcast. 'That would have been the most fantastic *Medic* show of all time.'[120] Sid Luft had been persuaded to get the doctors to allow a television crew into Judy's room for her to make an acceptance speech should she, as was expected, win the Oscar. However, because Warner Bros regarded the film as a flop, they did not buy any advertising in the trade press to promote the film. It was also believed that the cutting of almost half an hour of film would harm Judy's chances. The other nominees were Dorothy Dandridge for *Carmen Jones*, Audrey Hepburn for *Sabrina*, Grace Kelly in *The Country Girl* and Jane Wyman in *Magnificent Obsession*.

William Holden presented the Best Actress Academy Award after winning the Best Actor gong the year before for *Stalag 17* (1953). That year he had not been allowed to make an acceptance speech so as he stood before the audience he began, 'As I was going to say last year … ' before emcee Bob Hope rushed over, whispered something to Holden and pointed at his watch. Holden then announced the winner of the 1954 Best Actress Academy Award was Grace Kelly for *The Country Girl*, the film in which they had both starred.

In her room in the Cedars of Lebanon the television crew began silently to dismantle their equipment. Judy was understandably upset. She, like most others, thought that she was going to win. Sid Luft had prepared his wife for victory arranging a buffet in her room plus shrimps, caviar and two bottles of iced champagne. When Holden made his announcement, Luft put his arms around Judy and said, 'Baby, fuck the Academy Awards, you've got yours in the incubator. Why, those sons of bitches, they'd give it to a fucking Jap who shot up Pearl Harbor, but they wouldn't give it to my baby.'[121] As the crew continued putting their gear away without so much as a word to Judy, Luft said, 'Forget it darling. Open the champagne. I have my own Academy Award.'[122]

The night that Judy lost the Oscar was also the one that she developed a series of phobias that left her unable to set foot on a movie sound stage again. *A Star is Born* may have won Judy critical acclaim but it did nothing to alleviate the financial burden she was under. Sid Luft decided that there was only one thing for it – Judy would have to return to the stage. The theatrical stage held as many fears for her as the cinematic one but Luft was insistent. Nowadays, Judy would probably have been diagnosed with post-natal depression but medical science was not so advanced more than 50 years ago. Judy needed her husband at her side as he had been the night she lost out to Grace Kelly for the Oscar. Instead, Luft left her at home with three young children under the age of 10 while he scoured the country looking for work. By this time, Judy's body had become tolerant of her pill abuse and although she was gobbling down slimming pills, the excess weight refused to budge.

Nine weeks after the birth of his son, Luft booked Judy into a seven-city West Coast tour and then arranged for her to appear at the New Frontier in Las Vegas. On 24 September 1955 she appeared in a 90-minute television special for *Ford Star Jubilee*. It was acclaimed by the press but any good feelings Judy may have had were quickly eaten up by the IRS who took most of her earnings for that year but still left her owing nearly $300,000.

Judy longed for Luft to be a proper husband but to no avail. She recalled, 'We were losing out ability to communicate with each other. I had learned how to handle an audience again, how to be an entertainer. But I didn't seem to be learning much from my marriage.'[123] When they were together arguments escalated into violence and Judy would find herself on the wrong end of Luft's fists. On 4 February 1956 Judy filed for divorce from Luft for the first time.

Judy rekindled a relationship with Frank Sinatra but it was one that was based mainly on sex, and oral sex at that. Although Judy had wanted David Rose to perform oral sex, she found giving it to Sinatra tiring. 'I'm worried about Frank. All he wants are blowjobs,' she told her friend and bedmate Harry Rubin.[124]

In September 1956 she again appeared at the Palace Theatre and was amazed to see a gold plaque had been erected that bore the legend 'This was the dressing room of Judy Garland who set the all-time long-run record, 16 October 1951–24 February 1952 RKO Palace Theatre'.[125] This time Judy did not received the uncritical acclaim that her last appearance at the Palace had generated. Her weight was certainly problematic and inhibited her movements. She was also not as comfortable with her general demeanour. It was approximately this time that the Garland Cult had its birth, especially among homosexuals who recognised a fellow tortured soul in Judy; someone who did not quite fit into the social milieu. Gays liked and like someone who has suffered before they pass on their adulation. Judy was certainly suffering. She suffered terribly from stage fright and such excessive hyperhydrosis that he had to change outfits several times during performances. When she came off she would reek of body odour and so would virtually bathe in Joy perfume to mask the smell. That had the effect, however, of making her feel sick during a performance when the perfume smell over-whelmed her.

On 4 March 1958, after a brief reconciliation, Judy again filed for divorce, claiming that Luft 'had beaten and attempted to strangle the plaintiff on many occasions the last being 21 February 1958'.[126] Reconciled, they again separated in January 1961 after a sabbatical in London. Things were going from bad to worse. On 25 March 1958 the State Tax Commission issued a tax warrant against Judy in New York over unpaid taxes. Eight days later, on 3 April, a further warrant was issued for Judy's arrest for non-payment of $8,000 in 1952 relating to her performance at the Palace Theatre. Luft, although he had taken all the moneys, had not seen to paying Judy's resultant tax bill. On New Year's Eve 1958 Judy appeared at the Flamingo Hotel in Las Vegas, Nevada. The audience was drunk and unappreciative of Judy's talents. After five songs she was heckled mercilessly. One patron shouted, 'Get outta here. You're too overweight and we don't want to hear you anyway.'[127] Again, Judy received poor publicity in the press and her public profile was not helped in January 1959 when a journalist, Marie Torres, wrote a story for the *New York Herald-Tribune* quoting an unnamed Columbia Broadcasting System executive as saying that Judy was 'known for a highly developed inferiority complex'. Judy sued CBS for libel and breach of contract claiming $1,393,333 and the judge ordered Torres to reveal her source. When she refused, as all good journalists should, she was sent to prison for ten days for contempt of court. The jailing did not endear the ladies and gentlemen of the Fourth Estate to Judy. The respected columnist Dorothy Kilgallen commented, 'I must say I'd never thought I'd live to see the day when anyone would be tossed into the jug for saying Judy Garland had problems.'[128] Later that year Judy was taken in great pain to Doctors' Hospital

Though she always smiled her way through trouble, Judy's struggle to control her weight was a constant torment. Photographed here in an interview in 1959

in New York where she was diagnosed as suffering from hepatitis. The medics who attended Judy told Luft that she might never perform again. It was a difficult situation for him: he stayed by her side at the hospital but always at the back of his mind was the thought that if Judy retired who would support the family? Matters became even more serious when Judy's condition weakened. Luft thought long and hard before he came up with an idea that could garner some money – Judy's life story would be sure to top the best-seller lists. He met with Bennett Cerf at Random House publishers and persuaded him to pay a $35,000 advance for Judy's book. Back at home Judy gave a few interviews to a ghostwriter but as her health improved she decided that she did not want to go ahead with the book. The material that was gathered was eventually sold to *McCall's* magazine.

Judy was the subject of much carping press coverage. They wrote about her weight and her supposed drinking and drug taking. It all became too much for her and she fell into a deep depression. As with many people she looked back on happier times and decided that she had been happy in England and had received courteous coverage from the English press. She would move to England, she decided, and Luft and the three children would accompany her.

Judy had been in England for six months when her financial chickens came home to roost, or rather the lack of financial chickens came home to roost. She and Luft had no money and, it seemed, no likelihood of any income. The only way to earn some money was by Judy performing once again on stage. In the autumn of 1960 she did just that, appearing in two concerts entitled *An Evening with Judy Garland*.

The concerts marked the beginning of the final end with Sid Luft. Judy sought new representation and signed with Freddie

Sid Luft and Judy managed to hide any personal anguish and pose as a happy family, with Liza, Lorna and Joey in Chelsea, London in 1960

Fields of Creative Management Associates. On 31 December 1960 Judy returned to New York – in the middle of one of the city's worst blizzards – without Luft. The marriage was over as she remembered, 'During that awful blizzard of January 1961 I went for a walk in the snow one night. I thought I was the blizzard. Suddenly I realised I didn't give a damn about him … for a few hours there it was difficult, like being shot out of a cannon. It was really terrifying.'[129]

Freddie Fields swung into action with his partner David Begelman to help alleviate Judy's financial situation. They settled a three-year long legal battle between Luft and CBS. They also arranged a schedule that would have stretched the patience of someone who was mentally and physically well. They arranged two television extravaganzas and then negotiated a cameo rôle in Stanley Kramer's *Judgment at Nuremberg* for which Judy would receive $50,000. She was also signed to use her vocal talents in an animated film entitled *Gay Purr-ee* plus she would star in two more films, *A Child is Waiting* and *I Could Go On Singing*, plus two separate concert tours totalling 48 performances in a year. It was an incredible feat but Judy managed it all – albeit with the help of vast quantities of pharmaceuticals. Judy's first concert was in Dallas, Texas, in February 1961, more than two and a half years before the city would become famous as the site of a presidential assassination. In essence the show was a more refined version of the one she had given in London the previous autumn. The show was a critical success – 'No entertainer has ever given such a show in Dallas,' reported one reviewer. Two nights later, she received four standing ovations in Houston.

A major gripe from Judy was that although she had made a great deal of money, both for herself and other people, she had never seen any of it. Fields and Begelman again came to the rescue. In her Dallas hotel room Judy was relaxing after the show when the two men arrived carrying a large brown paper bag. It was filled with money and to Judy's great delight they threw it into the air and allowed it to fall around her.

On 8 April Judy and Sid were invited to dinner at the home of Attorney-General Bobby Kennedy and did not get home until 4 a.m. Five hours later, the phone rang and the couple was invited to the White House where President Kennedy wanted to thank Judy for her support in the election.[130]

The last concert of the first tour was at Carnegie Hall, 57th Street and Seventh Avenue, on St George's Day, 1961 and it was to be recorded. Judy was, as usual, a bundle of nerves because the show was being recorded and because it included new material and she was always more comfortable with that which she knew. The acerbic bachelor, future critic and would-be actor Rex Reed was at the show and he recalled, 'I'd just come to New York and the thing I'd wanted to do all my life was see Judy Garland. I think it was probably the greatest experience I've ever had in the theatre. I had never seen that much love given to a performer. I had a marvellous seat – right next to Eli Wallach and Anne Jackson. [They] grabbed me. We were holding on to each other, and Tony Perkins was right in front of me; and Leonard [Bernstein] … even Hedda Hopper was there … and Lauren Bacall … they were all really with this lady. And it wasn't just her [hardcore] cult [fans] who supported her. This was show business and this was the hardest audience to please – really an audience of hard-nosed professional critics. It was the greatest triumph in anyone's life'.[131] Judy had lost more than two stone through the pressure of touring and when she appeared on stage she was the slim creature known to moviegoers. The show began with a rendition of *When You're Smiling* and everyone had grins on their

faces from that moment on until the first half ended with *That's Entertainment*. The second half lasted like the first three quarters of an hour. At the end of the show the audience virtually refused to leave Carnegie Hall and rushed the stage declaring their love for Judy.

Again the reviews were very favourable. The *New York Herald Tribune* reported, 'Judy Garland sang, let it be reported, as she hasn't sang in years – not at the Palace and not at the Met: she sang with the heart that has been her hallmark, but added to it a happy self-confidence that gives new quality and depth to her performance. It's a performance that deserves all the pre-commitment that her very name evokes.'[132] Judy's next job was the cameo as Irene Hoffman Wallner in *Judgment at Nuremberg*, a film about the German war trials after the Second World War. The film was described by one critic as 'an electrifying account … although a trifle stagy and long, it's still a gripping movie'[133] while *Variety* said 'Both Clift and Miss Garland bring great emotional force and conviction to their chores, he as a somewhat deranged victim of Nazi sterility measures, she as a German accused of relations with a Jew at a period when such an activity was forbidden and punishable by death for the Jew'.[134]

The Academy of Motion Picture Arts & Sciences agreed and Judy was nominated for a Best Supporting Actress Oscar for her performance as the middle-aged German gentile whose innocent friendship with an elderly Jew led to his execution and her imprisonment. Director Kramer said, 'She's a great technician. There's no one in the entertainment world today who can run the complete range of emotions from utter pathos to power the way she can. She knows how to laugh and to cry on cue.'[135]

Kramer had spent $150,000 on travel arrangements to get everyone to attend the première in West Berlin at which Willy

Back on glamorous form, Judy in her comeback concert in 1961

Brandt, the mayor, gave a speech. *Judgment at Nuremberg* was nominated for 11 Oscars: Best Film, Best Actor (Spencer Tracy and Maximilian Schell), Best Supporting Actor (Montgomery Clift), Best Supporting Actress (Judy), Best Director (Kramer), Best Screenplay (Abby Mann), Best Black and White Cinematography (Ernest Laszlo), Best Black and White Art Direction (Rudolph Sternad, George Milo), Best Editing (Frederic Knudtson) and Best Costumes (Jean Louis). On the big night, 9 April 1962, it won just two although Kramer was presented with the Irving G Thalberg Memorial Award. The presenter, ironically, was Judy's old MGM producer Arthur Freed. Whether by design or accident, Judy did not attend the ceremony at the Santa Monica Civic Auditorium. Joey Luft, whose birth had prevented Judy from attending the 1954 ceremony, came down with earache and Judy stayed with him at the Beverly Hills Hotel.[136] As it turned out, it was not to be Judy's night again. Rock Hudson presented the award to Rita Moreno for *West Side Story*.

Chapter 7

I Could Go On Singing

On 29 April 1962, less than three weeks after her Oscar disappointment, Judy filed for divorce from Luft who retaliated by threatening to have her declared an unfit mother. In September of the same year Judy again filed suit, this time in Las Vegas, Nevada, charging extreme mental cruelty. Luft returned fire, alleging that Judy had hidden $2 million of community property. A bitter custody battle ensued.

To film *A Child is Waiting*, a movie about mentally retarded children, Judy called upon her experiences in Peter Bent Brigham Hospital. Her co-star was Burt Lancaster and the film was shot in Pacific State Hospital in Pomona, California. All the children in the film, apart from the leading boy, were patients. When filming wrapped Judy was depressed and, without a man to comfort her, began ringing friends late at night. It was a similar pattern to Marilyn Monroe who was also an inveterate user of the telephone late at night. Judy recalled, 'I'm afraid at night. I didn't know how to use the phone when I was a scared little girl. But now at the age of 41, I do know how to use the phone and I make all these nocturnal calls to wake up all my friends about three in the morning.

I resent the fact that they're sleeping and they're not around here … It's almost like everybody were Mama, and everybody went away and I'm left alone.'

Judy was sent a script by Mayo Simon entitled *The Lonely Stage*. Under the title *I Could Go On Singing* it would be the last completed film that she made. Judy was slated to play the role of Jenny Bowman, a world-famous singer who was going through a traumatic period in her life, sacrificing her happiness for her career. The film was shot in England and Dirk Bogarde was hired to play her co-star, Dr David Donne.

As she was waiting to leave for London to begin filming, Judy was fearful that Sid Luft would try to snatch the children. She hired three bodyguards and they escorted her to Idlewild Airport on Long Island.[137] Liza was by this time studying at the New York High School of Performing Arts (later to be immortalised in the film and television series *Fame*).

In London Judy still did not feel safe and told journalists that she and Luft had been estranged for two years and their marriage was dead. Further, Judy moved to have Lorna and Joey made wards of court. Shortly before filming began Luft arrived in London. It did not bode well for a happy film set and so it proved. When the film began shooting cast and crew referred to Judy as 'Miss Garland'. Thanks to pills and pressure caused by Luft's presence they called her 'It' by the time the movie wrapped. The situation could have been so different. Judy and the terribly closeted homosexual Bogarde had met on 31 December 1956 at a party where his cigarette had accidentally burned a hole in her dress. Three years later, on 28 August 1960, he was in the audience of the London Palladium when she serenaded him with *It Never Was You* and *You Made Me Love You*. The notoriously private Bogarde hated every minute but kept a fixed smile on his face throughout.

On 13 July 1962 – two months into filming of *I Could Go On Singing* – Judy walked out of the production after a huge row. In one of his autobiographies, *Snakes and Ladders*, Bogarde devotes a page and a half to it. His lover, Tony Forwood, put the tantrum down to Judy not being loved enough. Eventually, after much diplomacy, Judy returned for the last fortnight to finish the film. *I Could Go On Singing* was probably the film that most realistically reflected the real Judy as opposed to the reel one. In one scene she tells David (Bogarde's character), 'There's an old

Life on the set of 'I Could Go On Singing' had been a nightmare, but both Judy and Dirk Bogarde managed to smile at the premiere in March 1963

Sir Dirk Bogarde (28 March 1921–8 May 1999) was born in Hampstead, north London as Derek Niven Van Den Bogaerde. He made his stage *début* in December 1939 in a play ironically entitled *When We Are Married*. Signed to a contract by Rank he played heavy dramas, light comedies and everything in between. He was acclaimed for his performance as Melville Farr, a gay lawyer, in Basil Dearden's *Victim* (1961) and won large audiences for his *Doctor …* films including *Doctor In The House* (1954), *Doctor At Sea* (1955), *Doctor At Large* (1956) and *Doctor In Distress* (1963) all as Simon Sparrow. He was the villain who shot and killed PC George Dixon in *The Blue Lamp* (1950). Bogarde was knighted in 1992. He died of a heart attack in London aged 78.

saying: When you go onstage, you don't feel any pain; and when the lights hit you, you don't feel anything … It's a stinking lie.' The film – her last celluloid experience – was a flop.

On 4 August 1962 Judy's friend Marilyn Monroe died of a drugs overdose. She was just 36 years old, four years younger than Judy. 'I knew Marilyn Monroe and loved her dearly. She asked me for help. Me! I didn't know what to tell her. One night at a party at Clifton Webb's house, Marilyn followed me from room to room. "I don't want to get too far away from you," she said. "I'm scared." I told her, "We're all scared. I'm scared too."'[138] At Marilyn's funeral *Somewhere Over The Rainbow* was played. Marilyn's death brought about another bout of depression for Judy. She said, 'I don't think Marilyn really meant to harm herself. It was partly because she had too many pills available, then was deserted by her friends. You shouldn't be told you're completely irresponsible and be left alone with too much medication. It's too easy to forget. You take a couple of sleeping pills and you wake up in 20 minutes and forget you've taken them. So you take a couple more, and, the next thing you know, you've taken too many.'[139]

On 15 September 1962 Judy was discovered unconscious in her room and taken to Carson-Tahoe Hospital where her life was saved by the hospital's chief of staff Dr Richard Grundy. In his examination of Judy he discovered that she was suffering from acute pyelonephritis of the right kidney. Grundy told the press that Judy had taken an accidental overdose because of the pain she was suffering from her infected kidney. In February 1963 while appearing a in a production of *Carnival* at the Mineola Playhouse in New York the hotel chambermaid discovered Judy unconscious by the side of her bed with cuts on her face. She was taken to Mount Sinai Hospital and the first editions of the next day's newspapers reported another suicide attempt. Her doctors claimed that Judy had only fallen over. A few days later, Judy and Sid Luft were back together again and flew to London for the première of *I Could Go On Singing*. They returned to New York and watched Liza in her professional debut in *Flora, the Red Menace*. Once more Judy was found unconscious in her hotel room (in the St Regis) and once more the press announced another suicide attempt. Again, the doctors tried to cover claiming that Judy was merely suffering from exhaustion. Sid Luft again began to exert pressure on Judy's career. Fields and Begelman were her agents but he was her manager (and, let's not forget, still her husband). Judy appeared at Harrah's in Lake Tahoe but collapsed after a week and was replaced by Mickey Rooney. She then flew to England where she appeared on *Sunday Night at the London Palladium* but twice missed song cues and then tried to leave the stage the wrong way. Judy returned to America to do another television show that was not quite as excruciating as the one at the Palladium but once again it looked like the wheels were coming off Judy's career.

On 29 September 1963 CBS took a chance and launched *The Judy Garland Show*, a weekly hour-long programme broadcast from 7800 Beverly Boulevard in Hollywood. Judy was paid $30,000 per show but after taxes, agents and managerial percentages were deducted she was left with around $3,250 per week. The music was arranged by Mel Tormé, much to Judy's horror. He wanted to feature a regular selection of new material while Judy preferred to rely on the standards that had seen her through numerous stage shows. The programme was produced by George Schlatter, later to find a measure of fame as the producer of *Rowan & Martin's Laugh-In*.

The first guest star was Donald O'Connor with Jerry van Dyke supporting. He was to appear nine times in total on the series.[140]

Jack Gould, the television critic of the *New York Times*, was not impressed by the show although his criticisms were aimed at CBS and not personally at Judy. 'The busybodies got so in the way that the singer never had the chance to sing as only she can. To call the hour a grievous disappointment would be to miss the point. It was an absolute mystery ... The thinking of CBS executives was to develop a "new" Judy, one who would indulge in light banter and make way for suitable guests to share the weekly tasks ... Those telephones on the 20th floor of CBS's home should buzz this morning with but one directive to Hollywood – Free Judy.'[141]

A watching viewer was more impressed. He telegrammed, 'Congratulations on a wonderful show last night. Know it will be a big hit in the coming season. John F Kennedy'.[142] Judy also claimed that JFK had told her that the White House had changed its Sunday dinner schedule to allow the President to watch the show.[143]

As was the case on many of her film sets, Judy did not endear herself to the crew. She was often late on set but defended herself, 'I haven't missed any rehearsals – if I had, I wouldn't have been able to do the show. There's just no time to indulge yourself on weekly television – you don't even have time to get a headache or catch a cold.'[144] She was addicted to speed and was on a strict diet to remain slim for the cameras. She was also insecure because television was a relatively new medium and her experience was in live theatre and films. She was also suffering from severe physical pain. Although she drank little alcohol, the combination of it with uppers and downers led many to believe that she was permanently drunk. The apparent inebriation did not stop a fling with the actor Glenn Ford but the affair ended when the series did. The show was dropped after one season of 26 episodes.

Immediately following the cancellation of *The Judy Garland Show*, Judy was booked on a concert tour of Australia and the Far East that began in Melbourne. Judy did not have an agent or manager to accompany her on the long, arduous journey. The gay actor Roddy McDowall had recently introduced Judy to one of his friends, a twentysomething wannabe actor named Mark Herron, who was to become her fourth husband. Keeping things in the family, Herron would have an affair with Peter Allen whom Judy would meet on the tour and who would go on to marry Liza Minnelli. He was also a lover of Charles Laughton. Judy asked Herron to be her tour manager but the press sniggeringly referred to him as her 'travelling companion'. Little did they know that Herron's interest in Judy, while no doubt profound and sincere, was not sexual.

The journey to Melbourne took 19 hours and to keep awake for her scheduled meetings Judy took an extra large dose of amphetamines. It kept her awake but had the side effect of making her unsteady on her feet and she was 67 minutes late for her gig at the Festival Hall on 20 May. The 7,000-strong audience was not pleased at being kept waiting and when Judy stumbled on stage they assumed that she was drunk and began bellowing at her. Judy called out, 'I love you, too' but the audience would not be assuaged. 'Get on with it. Sing something! Have another brandy,' they yelled.[145] Judy did just that for 45 minutes but it was too late. The Australian audience could not be won over and finally Judy put the microphone down and simply walked off stage. The next show was scheduled for Sydney and the show went off without a hitch. To avoid being late for her next stop in Hong Kong, Judy flew on 23 May into the British colony four days before the 90mph winds of Typhoon Viola hit on 27/28 May 1964. Judy retired to her room alone. Some hours later Mark Herron called in to check on her and found Judy comatose. She was rushed to hospital where doctors worked feverishly on her but Judy remained unconscious for 15 long, worrying hours. Herron was not allowed to see her and he began weeping, begging reporters to alert Freddie Fields. Various rumours sprung up around the incident including the inevitable suicide attempt or possibly a heart attack. Dr Lee Siegel flew in from Hollywood at Fields's suggestion. He diagnosed pleurisy and prescribed lots of rest and relaxation. For much of her life Judy had fought a battle with her weight, but in the last few years she had the exact opposite problem. She struggled to maintain her weight. At the time of this latest collapse, Judy weighed less than six stone.

On 11 June Judy and Herron went nightclubbing and told everyone that they had married on 6 June, five days earlier. The 'ceremony' had been performed by a Scandinavian captain aboard a boat in Hong Kong harbour. The little matter that Judy was still legally married to Sid Luft did not appear to concern the newlyweds. When they returned to Los Angeles Luft filed a child custody suit claiming that Judy was 'emotionally disturbed and unbalanced'. He also mentioned in the suit that Judy attempted to kill herself more than 20 times.

Meanwhile, while Judy was away on tour her, her sister Suzy committed suicide at the age of 48 with a drugs overdose in Las Vegas, Nevada, on 26 May 1964.

Judy was again hospitalised at the Cedars of Lebanon a week after her return suffering from abdominal pains. Released, Judy and Herron travelled to Copenhagen and then London where once again Judy found herself in hospital, this time St Stephen's, with cuts to her wrists caused, so she claimed, by opening a trunk with a knife.

In London Judy was invited to appear in the midnight charity revue *Night of a Hundred Stars* at the London Palladium on 23 July 1964 in aid of the Combined Theatrical Charities Appeals Council.[146] Her doctors expressly forbade Judy to appear but she ignored them and arrived at the theatre door in Argyle Street. She informed the show's director that while she was happy to appear there was no way that she could sing. She would merely walk on stage, say a few words and take a bow before making a graceful exit. That was the plan. That was not what happened.

Following an electric performance by The Beatles Judy walked onto the Palladium stage. There was an immediate ovation and people cried out 'Sing, Judy, sing'. Tears came into Judy's eyes as she looked at her fans. The audience begged for *Somewhere over the Rainbow* but Judy shook her head and began to back off the stage. The cheers became louder and Judy walked slowly to centre stage. Then silence fell and the crowd waited with baited breath.

The orchestra struck up the familiar strains of Judy's virtual theme song. The rendition was poignant in the extreme and when Judy had finished, the audience enveloped her in love and enthusiasm. They demanded an encore and Judy sang *Swanee*. Shirley Bassey had been due to follow Judy but such was the feeling in the auditorium that there was no alternative but to end the show and cancel Bassey's slot.

Happy to be among her adoring fans, Judy stayed in London for the summer and basked in their adulation. Herron was a different matter and Judy complained that she never saw him. On 24 September Judy was once again suffering from mysterious abdominal pains and was admitted to a nursing home. While she was in London Sid Luft's lawsuit that claimed that Judy was an unfit mother came to court in Santa Monica, California. The portrait painted of Judy by Luft's legal team was not a pretty one. She was labelled a drunk and a drug addict with self-destructive

Judy and her fourth husband Mark Herron out walking the wilder side of London's night life, with club owners Reggie and Ronnie Kray

tendencies. Luft also claimed that Judy was squandering their children's inheritance on Mark Herron. Despite all the mud-slinging the judge decided that Judy should retain custody of the children.

On 9 September 1964 Liza flew to London and on 8 November she appeared onstage with her mother at the London Palladium. Liza had taken some persuading to appear at the show and given the reaction, Judy almost certainly wished that she had not bothered. Judy sang ten songs alone, Liza eight and they duetted on 12 more. Judy felt herself upstaged by her daughter and began attempting to regain the initiative. She spoke over Liza's lines and at one stage even attempted to push her off the stage. One critic opined, 'At times one had the incredible sensation of seeing and hearing in Liza the Judy Garland of 25 years ago.'[147] As the two women left the stage, Judy told Liza to go to her dressing room but Liza turned and saw her mother heading for the stage to take another bow. Liza ran after her mother and both women took the applause. They were never to work together again. It was probably the last time that Judy's voice and health were strong enough to be able to sustain an entire concert. Returning to America for a tour, she was often ill at ease during performances and at one concert in Cincinnati, Ohio, she had to leave the stage mid-concert because she was so ill.

On 5 April 1965 Judy appeared at the Oscar ceremony held at the Santa Monica Civic Auditorium and sang a medley of Cole Porter songs although her voice was not what it once was. Still, the audience urged her on to succeed and she did not disappoint. On 11 May 1965 Judy, wearing black chiffon and diamonds, was in the audience when Liza opened at the Alive Theatre in her Tony-award winning musical *Flora, the Red Menace*. She had sent a telegram, 'My darling baby, I know you will be brilliant as always tonight. Don't be scared, just get out there and kill them. I love you, Momma.'[148] That night Judy, Liza and Vincente Minnelli celebrated at Ruby Foo's and mother and daughter sang together. It was also the first time that she had refused a fan an autograph, 'No, this is Liza's night.'[149] On 19 May 1965 in Santa Monica the Lufts were finally divorced. On 13 June 1965 Judy was once again ill and admitted to the Neuropsychiatric Institute of the University of California at Los Angeles. The press was told that Judy had suffered a 'nervous collapse'. Judy had been booked

Following his divorce from Judy, Sid Luft married Patti Hemingway in 1970 but that ended in divorce. On 20 March 1993 he married the actress Camille Keaton, 35 years his junior. She is the great-niece of Buster Keaton and is best known for her role in the long-banned film *I Spit On Your Grave* (1978) in which she takes a gruesome revenge against the four men who raped her. In September 2002 a Los Angeles District judge forbade Luft from selling the replacement Juvenile Oscar Judy had received in 1940. Luft was further ordered to pay nearly $60,000 to The Academy of Motion Picture Arts and Sciences in settlement of their lawsuit against him for repeatedly trying to sell the statuette.

119

to appear at the Greek Theatre in Los Angeles and was determined not to let her fans down. The day of the show dawned and
Judy psyched herself up to appear, only to trip over one of her
dogs and break her arm. Ever the trouper Judy went on but had
to curtail the show when the pain became too intense. It was her
old childhood friend Mickey Rooney who stepped up the plate
and finished the show for Judy.

On 14 November 1965 at 1.30 a.m. Judy married Mark Herron
at the Little Chapel of the West in Las Vegas. They were together
less than six months after the ceremony. On 3 August 1966 he
filed for maintenance support rather than divorce and claimed
that he hoped for a reconciliation. Two days later, Judy issued a
statement which read, 'His public and private behaviour, which
has been distasteful and untenable, makes any reconciliation
impossible.'[150] On 16 August Herron filed for divorce. Less than
a month later, on 12 September, Judy sought to have the marriage
annulled on the grounds of non-consummation. Her petition
was denied. The divorce was finally granted on 11 April 1967. Judy
claimed that Herron drank and hit and kicked her. It was also at
that point that Judy legally changed her name from Frances Ethel
Gumm to Judy Garland.

In 1966 she met Mickey Deans who was then manager of the
small nightclub Arthur on East 54th Street, which was owned
by Sybil Burton Christopher (the ex-wife of the actor Richard),
Roddy McDowall and the dancer Edward Vilella. (Arthur which
could legally only accommodate 174 people was open from 1965
until 1970.) Deans had formerly been the pianist at Jilly's, the
nightclub owned by Frank Sinatra's friend Jilly Rizzo. It was an
odd introduction – Deans was asked to deliver drugs to Judy at
the St Regis Hotel, in New York. Lorna and Joey Luft opened the
door to the suite and Deans saw Judy standing behind them. As

*Judy attended Liza's opening
night at the Cocoanut Grove
nightclub in November 1965.
Mark Herron looks in from the
left of the picture while actor
George Hamilton peers over
Judy's head*

she walked to the door to greet him, she tripped over an ottoman and fell flat on her face. Judy was now on an irreversible downward spiral. Her addiction to drugs was out of control. Her financial situation was again dire. Her body was gradually shutting down.

In early 1967 Judy was back at the St Regis Hotel in New York. Liza was going to marry her first gay husband. On 1 March Twentieth Century-Fox announced that Judy had been cast in the film version of Jacqueline Susann's scandalous novel about drugs *Valley of the Dolls*. Judy was to play Helen Lawson, 'an ageing queen of Broadway musicals who had the talent to get to the top – and had the claws to stay there'.[151] Judy would be paid $75,000 for about 10 days' work. As part of her press duties, she gave an interview to John Gruen of the *New York Herald Tribune* who asked her how she felt about being labelled a legend. 'If I'm a legend, then why am I so lonely?'[152] was her plaintive response.

When Judy left New York for more work on the film she was accompanied by her new lover Tom Green, a publicist who the press were referring to as her 'fiancé'. (Judy would have him arrested for grand larceny on 11 April 1967.) On the film set, however, she felt uncomfortable and believed that the film was 'dirty' and often would not turn up on set when scenes of that ilk were being filmed. 'That very strange Jacqueline Susann doesn't seem to know any words with more than four letters,' she complained, 'I just can't stomach it.'[153]

Judy asked to be released from her contract and when Twentieth Century-Fox refused, Judy simply did not turn up on set. Eventually on 24 April 1967, the corporation sacked her but had to pay her $40,000 compensation. She was replaced by Susan Hayward.

On 8 June 1967, at Sid Luft's urging, she signed a contract

with Group V Limited. The five, Judy was led to believe, consisted of Judy, Liza, Lorna, Joey and Sid Luft. The ideas was that Group V would be Judy's agents and management representatives, and arrange her future financial security. In fact, Group V was a company owned by a friend of Luft called Raymond Filiberti, 38, who had been to prison for transporting stolen securities across state lines. All of Judy's earnings were channelled into Group V but she saw little of the money and once her luggage was held by a hotel after Group V failed to meet her hotel bill. It is incredible that if Luft had Judy's best interests at heart that he allowed her to sign the contract. In effect, Judy belonged to Group V from the date of the signature and whatever path her career took it would be to the benefit of Group V, not Judy. Clause 13 of the contract forbade Judy from talking to the press without express permission from Group V. Clause 17 even held Judy financially responsible for any concerts that she might miss unless she gave 24 hours' notice. On 29 December 1968 Judy gave a deposition to the Queen's Bench Division of the High Court of Justice in which she outlined how she had been conned by Group V.

On 19 May 1968 to cover a debt of $18,750 Luft loaned for 90 days for the sum of $1 Judy's Group V contract to Leon J Greenspan and Howard Harper (né Harker; he had a criminal record for violence). Judy was furious and refused to perform at any scheduled concerts unless she was paid by 4 p.m. of the day of the concert. Luft jotted an agreement to that effect on 26 June 1968 on the stationery of the Hotel Berkeley-Carteret in Asbury Park, New Jersey.

Not long afterwards, Judy told reporters that she would like to appear in a Broadway musical but it was a pipe dream. Her health and drug addiction would never have permitted it.

In June 1968 in a desperate bid to get help, Judy flew to

Massachusetts (on someone's else's shilling) and booked herself into the Peter Bent Brigham Hospital in Boston.

Judy's relationship with Tom Green came to an end and on 24 October 1968 she met John Meyer, a pub singer, who was to write a 322-page book about his two months with her. The relationship lead to Judy's final record, her version of his song *I'd Like To Hate Myself In The Morning*. On 28 October 1968 Luft had not repaid the loan so Harper and Greenspan filed suit in the Supreme Court of Westchester County, New York for the permanent transfer of Judy Garland, her talents and earnings.

Back from Boston Judy once again took up with Mickey Deans. They saw a lot of each other, meeting after shows or when his discotheque closed. They would go to an all-night supermarket at five in the morning and Judy would sit in the trolley like a small child while Deans pushed it around the aisles.

With Deans's encouragement Judy agreed to a month's residence at the Talk of the Town in London on the corner of Charing Cross Road and Leicester Square. When Luft heard, he told Judy that he owned the arrangements of all her songs and would not allow her to use them unless he was paid. Deans came to the rescue, telling Judy to 'tell Luft to fuck it' and that he would get new arrangements for her to use. On 28 December 1968 they flew to London.

Chapter 8

The End of the Rainbow

As Judy cleared customs she was presented with a writ issued by Greenspan and Harper that was seeking to restrain her from opening at the Talk of the Town on 30 December. On that day Judy appeared before Mr Justice Magarry to answer the writ. He read through the contract and delivered his verdict. 'This transaction is one which I would not enjoin a dog. Certainly, I would not enjoin Miss Garland.' He dismissed the case and ordered Greenspan and Harper to pay all the costs of the action, around £1,000.

At 11.15 p.m. Judy opened the show and promptly forgot her words and, much to her annoyance, her musical director Burt Rhodes prompted her.

Despite the success she was enjoying, Judy missed her younger children and was still heavily dependent on pills. A doctor who prescribed some pills in those early days of 1969 remembers that Judy had a body odour problem which even her perfume (Ma Griffe) could not conceal.

On 9 January 1969 she and Deans had their relationship blessed in St Marylebone Parish, the same church that Robert

Browning had married Elizabeth Barrett. Judy's run at the Talk of the Town ended on Saturday 1 February 1969. On 19 February she appeared on *Sunday Night at the London Palladium*. Deans and Judy moved into 4 Cadogan Lane, Chelsea, a mews house abutting Sloane Avenue in Belgravia.

On 15 March 1969 at Chelsea Registry Office Judy and Deans were married by M A Lawrence. Judy had now been married five times and three of her husbands – Minnelli, Herron and Deans – were homosexual. The wedding breakfast was held at Quaglino's.

Judy travelled to Scandinavia to fulfil a three-date concert tour in Malmo and Stockholm in Sweden and Copenhagen in Denmark arranged by Deans. Judy's last ever concert took place at the Falkoner Center in Copenhagen on 25 March. The couple returned to London and a rainstorm. Three months later, Judy Garland was dead.

On 21 June 1969 Judy and Deans were at their home, with Deans's close friend Philip Roberge watching the documentary about the House of Windsor, *The Royal Family*, when Judy and her husband began an argument. She ran into the street shouting and after a time he went after her. Unable to find her he returned to the house and went to bed. At approximately 10.40am the next morning the telephone rang for Judy. Deans scoured the house and discovered the bathroom door was locked. He banged on it but received no reply. He climbed in through the bathroom window and found a naked Judy dead, sitting on the lavatory. Rigor mortis had already set in. She was only 47. The official cause of death was given as 'Barbiturate Poisoning (quinalbarbitone), incautious self-overdosage, accidental.'

Following an autopsy performed by Dr Gavin Thurston at Westminster Hospital her corpse was taken back to America three days later. On 26 and 27 June her body lay in state at Frank E

It is one of life's strange coincidences that 27 June 1969 – the day that Judy's body was lying in state – is regarded as the birth of the gay rights movement. It was the date of the first Stonewall Riot in New York. Nine plainclothes policemen went to the Stonewall Inn at 53 Christopher Street in Greenwich Village to close the bar for selling alcohol without a licence. After some arrests were made a crowd gathered and the police were forced to barricade themselves in the bar until help arrived. The riot lasted less than 45 minutes but the following night violence again broke out at the Stonewall Inn. A writer later commented, 'Judy's death inspired those Stonewall queens.'

Judy looking frail and gaunt at her last ever stage performance in Copenhagen in March 1969

More than 20,000 people queued on Madison Avenue to pay a last homage to Judy at the Frank. E. Campbell Funeral home in Manhattan in June 1969

Campbell's Funeral Home, 1076 Madison Avenue, New York and almost 22,000 fans paid homage to her. A moving funeral service followed with James Mason delivering a 20-minute eulogy. The other mourners included Harold Arlen, Lauren Bacall, Jack Benny, Ray Bolger, Sammy Davis Jr, Katharine Hepburn, Burt Lancaster, Patricia Kennedy Lawford, Dean Martin, Otto Preminger, Kay Thompson and Lana Turner.

The coffin was then taken to Ferncliff Cemetery and Mausoleum, Secor Road, Hartsdale, New York 10530, where it was placed in a temporary crypt awaiting her family's instructions. In October Mickey Deans wrote, 'I decided she would be buried in a quiet peaceful cemetery outside New York … She was buried with all the jewellery she wore at our wedding.'[154] The problem was that Judy had not been 'buried with all the jewellery'. She had not been buried at all. More than a year after her death, she was still in the temporary crypt, her only remembrance a three-inch plastic nametag bearing the legend 'Judy Garland Deans'. The crypts were free for 60 days after death but then the family was charged $20 per month. The shameful behaviour of her family was exposed in the *National Enquirer* and finally on 4 November 1970 Judy Garland was laid to rest in Mausoleum Unit 9, Section HH, Crypt 31 at Ferncliff.

Marcella Rabwin was later asked if she had any regrets about helping Judy on the road to stardom. Her answer was definite. 'For having given the world that great talent? No.'

Epilogue

Over the Rainbow
– The Finale

Mary Jane 'Suzy' Gumm married twice. Her first husband was the musician Lee Kahn (some say Cahn) on 24 September 1935, her 20th birthday. Her second husband was Jack Cathcart. In Las Vegas, Nevada, on 26 May 1964 she committed suicide at the age of 48 with a drugs overdose.

Dorothy Virginia 'Jimmy' Gumm died in Dallas, Texas on 27 May 1977. She, too, had been twice married, to the musician Bobby Sherwood in 1936 by whom she had a daughter Judy Gail (unsurprisingly, the child's name was changed and she became Judalein) in May 1938 and musical arranger Johnny Thompson in 1948.

Mark Herron died on 13 January 1996 aged 67 in Los Angeles of cancer. He was for a long time the lover of the character actor Henry Brandon (1912–90).

Joey Luft works as a scenic photographer.

Lorna Luft has never eclipsed the fame of either her mother or half-sister, although her private life has been somewhat more settled. Judy believed that the major star in the next generation of her family would be Lorna. She began carving out her own career early, landing a role in Hal David and Neil Simon's *Promises, Promises* on Broadway in 1971, after studying at the Banff School of Fine Arts. She then worked as a backup for Blondie, appeared in films, recorded several albums of movie and musical theatre standards and performed concerts around the world. In 2003 she began singing her mother's songs in concert. 'It takes you a long time to deal with your legacy because there's no book in any library that tells you how to deal with it.' She will not, however, sing *Somewhere Over the Rainbow*. She regularly appears in concerts on both sides of the Atlantic and was on stage two days after the memorial service for her father from whom she was estranged. She has been married twice. Her first husband was rock star Jake Hooker by whom she has a son, Jesse Cole (b. April 1984), and a daughter, Vanessa Jade (b. September 1990). They were married at St Bartholomew's Church, London on 14 February 1977. The Rev Peter Delaney who had married Judy and Mickey Deans and then officiated at Judy's funeral performed the ceremony. Lorna married musician Colin Freeman on 14 September 1996.

Sid Luft died of a heart attack in Santa Monica on 15 September 2005. He was 89. He was survived by his fourth wife, an actress almost four decades his junior. Luft fell out with daughter Lorna over her book *Me and My Shadows: A Family Story*. He was further distraught by the 2001 film made of Lorna's book. 'There were so many lies in that movie,' he told one reporter. 'I never mismanaged Judy's money – Lorna was only 15 when her mother died, so what the hell did she really know about what went on? Whatever bad things happened, you don't fall out of love with somebody like Judy. All I know is that, if anyone tried to save a woman who was breaking apart, I did. I did the best I could do, and it still wasn't enough.' His fourth wife, the actress Camille Keaton, three children and his stepdaughter, Liza, survived him.

Louis B Mayer suffered a kidney infection in October 1957 and on the 28th fell into a coma. He died at 12.35 a.m. the next day aged 72. He was buried in The Chapel Mausoleum's Corridor of Immortality in Home of Peace Memorial Park, 4334 Whittier Boulevard, Los Angeles, California 90023. His funeral was well attended and supposedly gave rise to two stories. Samuel Goldwyn reportedly said, 'The reason so many people turned up at his funeral is that they wanted to make sure the son of a bitch was dead.' The other was the comment 'Give the people what they want and they will turn up for it.'

Liza Minnelli has created more headlines in recent years through her private life than her professional one despite winning an Oscar (for *Cabaret* in 1972), three Tonys (for *Flora, the Red Menace* (it ran from 11 May until 24 July 1965), Winter Garden Show (1974) and *The Act* (1978)), an Emmy (for the TV special *Liza with a Z* in 1972) and a Golden Globe (for *A Time to Live* in 1985). On 3 March 1967 in New York City she married the gay entertainer Peter Allen. Three weeks later, she found him in bed with another man. They divorced on 24 July 1974 and he died from AIDS on 18 June 1992. She married Jack Haley, Jr, the son of her mother's *Wizard of Oz* co-star, on 15 September 1974 and they divorced in April 1979. On 4 December 1979 she married Mark Gero but they were divorced on 27 January 1992. Perhaps her most bizarre wedding was on 16 March 2002 to David Gest in a ceremony at which Michael Jackson was best man and Elizabeth Taylor a bridesmaid. The couple announced their separation on 25 July 2003. She has been in rehab on several occasions.

Vincente Minnelli died of Alzheimer's Disease aged 83 at his home on North Crescent Drive, in Beverly Hills, California.

Mickey Rooney continues to act.

David Rose died in Burbank, California aged 80 in 1990.

Notes

1. Some sources say 5ft 9in.
2. Gerold Frank, *Judy* (Da Capo, New York: 1999) p 6.
3. Gerald Clarke, *Get Happy: The Life of Judy Garland* (TimeWarner, London: 2001), p 14.
4. Some sources say that it was the Orpheum Theatre.
5. Frank, *Judy*, p 7.
6. Frank, *Judy*, p 7.
7. Frank, *Judy* p 11.
8. Frank, *Judy* p 16.
9. Clarke, *Get Happy*, p 19.
10. Clarke, *Get Happy*, p 40.
11. Clarke, *Get Happy*, p 42.
12. Shirley Temple also studied at the school.
13. Anne Edwards, *Judy Garland* (Corgi Books, London: 1976) p 22.
14. Frank, *Judy*, p 35.
15. Clarke, *Get Happy*, p 51.
16. Clarke, *Get Happy*, p 52.
17. Other students included Donald O'Connor, Marjorie Champion, Frankie Darro, Bonita Granville and Gloria DeHaven.

18. The St Valentine's Day Massacre was featured in the film *Some Like It Hot* (1959) which starred Tony Curtis, Jack Lemmon and Judy's friend Marilyn Monroe.

19. Clarke, *Get Happy*, p 48.

20. Frank, *Judy*, p 51.

21. Some authorities believe that Judy was, in fact, named after the character played by Carole Lombard in the film *Twentieth Century*, Lily Plotka, who changed her name to Lily Garland. Others insist that the name came about after Jessel said that the three sisters were as pretty 'as a garland of flowers'.

22. Oliver Hardy was known to family and friends as Babe.

23. Edwards, *Judy Garland*, p 27.

24. The original Cal-Neva (so called because it was on the California-Nevada border at 2, State Line, Crystal Bay, Lake Tahoe) was built in 1926 by wealthy San Francisco businessman Robert P Sherman, who used the Lodge as a guest house for his friends and real estate clients. The Cal Neva Lodge burned to the ground on 17 May 1937 but was rebuilt in just over 30 days by Norman Biltz and Adler Larson. It was owned by Frank Sinatra from 1960 until 1963 and became infamous as a Mafia hangout. In fact it was the presence of Mafioso Sam 'Momo' Giancana that cost Sinatra his gaming licence. It was also the location of Marilyn Monroe's 'lost weekend'. On 28–29 July 1962 Marilyn spent a weekend at the Cal-Neva but stories vary as to what exactly happened there. Some say that Marilyn spent the time in a drink- and drug-induced haze. Or, she spent the time with Joe Di Maggio and they resumed their relationship. Or, Marilyn attempted suicide and was found just in time. Those who are convinced that Marilyn did

indeed kill herself a week later believe this. Others believe that she spent the weekend with Giancana. For 20 years until December 1985, the Cal-Neva was neglected. The Cal Neva Resort (as it is now called) opened in February 1986 and is an impressive, full-service destination resort, featuring 200 lake view rooms, cabins, chalets and a casino.

25. Frank, *Judy*, p 60.
26. MGM boasted that it had 'more stars than there are in the heavens'. The studio employed more than 4,000 people. It had its own police force, fire station, telephone exchange, zoo and stables. It had 10 miles of road spaced over 180 acres.
27. Edens, who was a homosexual, and Kay Thompson, who was to become Judy's close friend and lesbian lover, shared the same birthday, 9 November. Edens was born in 1905 and died of cancer on 13 July 1970. Thompson was born three years later and died in New York on 2 July 1998.
28. Frank, *Judy*, p 46.
29. Edwards, *Judy Garland*, p 26.
30. Frank, *Judy*, p 80.
31. Edwards, *Judy Garland*, p 39.
32. *McCall's*, April 1957.
33. Clarke, *Get Happy*, p 67.
34. Edwards, *Judy Garland*, p 49.
35. Frank, *Judy*, p 83.
36. Leonard Maltin, *Leonard Maltin's Classic Movie Guide* (Plume, New York: 2005) p 434.
37. Frank, *Judy*, p 86.
38. *The New York Times*, 14 November 1936.
39. Frank, *Judy*, p 88.

40. Edwards, *Judy Garland*, p 49.

41. Edwards, *Judy Garland*, p 49.

42. Edwards, *Judy Garland*, p 50.

43. This was the day that Jane Fonda was born.

44. Maltin, *Maltin's Classic Movie Guide*, p 165.

45. *The New York Times*, 24 November 1938.

46. Rooney dated Turner before he married Gardner, who
was four inches taller, on 10 January 1942 in a small
Presbyterian church in the foothills of the Santa Ynez
Mountains. That night Ava lost her virginity to him.
Despite the fact that he was something of a playboy
Rooney was nervous as he undressed for bed – he put his
legs into the arms of his pyjamas! His bride was terrified
– her mother had warned her that sex was terrible and
had to be endured and not enjoyed. However, once Ava
got over her initial shyness she found she actually enjoyed
the event and looked forward to a repeat performance. It
was not to be – Rooney was a golf fanatic and made for
the green after breakfast. Ava wised up to Mickey within
a short time and ditched him. They divorced on 21 May
1943.

47. Morgan began costume fittings in mid-November 1938.
On 17 November 1938 (while the scenes in the Tin Man's
forest were being shot), Morgan tested his Professor
Marvel makeup on the set, using the same costume he had
worn for his Wizard test shots the day before. The costume
department bought half a dozen coats and jackets for
Morgan to try on. Together with the costumier, Morgan
and Victor Fleming picked a Prince Albert jacket 'ratty
with age' that had turned green. One hot day Morgan
began searching the pockets and came across the name 'L

Frank Baum', the author of six books about the land of Oz. The crew contacted the tailor in Chicago and he sent a notarised letter saying that the coat had been made for Frank Baum. Baum's widow identified the coat, too, and after the picture was finished it was presented it to her. Morgan made his first appearance before the cameras on 14 January 1939.

48. At the start of the film Auntie Em (Clara Blandick) is counting chickens: 'Sixty-seven, sixty-eight, sixty-nine' then puts a further three in her apron and takes one from Dorothy saying 'Seventy'. It should have been 73. On the table by the window was an oil lamp but it disappears before the window is blown open in the storm. Look when the bed is moving around the room during the tornado. Although the pictures on the wall move, the bottles on the table stay where they are. Dorothy's hair changes length at least three times. When Dorothy is taken to the Wicked Witch's castle her hair is mid-length. When Toto runs away her hair hangs down to her waist but when the Witch is turned into an hourglass her hair is shoulder length. When the Scarecrow (Ray Bolger) receives a brain he states: 'The sum of the square roots of any two sides of an isosceles triangle is equal to the square root of the remaining side.' Actually, it is not. In Pythagorean theory the square of the length of the hypotenuse of a right triangle is equal to the sum of the squares of the lengths of the other two sides.

49. Edwards, *Judy Garland*, p 62.

50. For many years there has been a rumour that a Munchkin hanged himself on the set during the filming after a Munchkiness spurned his advances, and that his death

was captured on-camera and used in the final print. It supposedly occurs at the very end of the Tin Man sequence, as Dorothy, the Scarecrow and the Tin Man head down the road on their way to the Emerald City. The story is absolute nonsense. In a bid to bring some life to an indoor shot scene the producers borrowed some birds from the Los Angeles Zoo. At the very end of this sequence, as the trio move off down the road and away from the camera, one of the larger birds (often said to be an emu, but more likely a crane) standing at the back of the set moves around and spreads its wings. No Munchkin, no hanging – merely a big bird. Logistically, it would have been impossible for the creature to be a Munchkin. Firstly, the forest scenes in *The Wizard of Oz* were filmed before the Munchkinland scenes, and so none of the actors playing the Munchkins would have been on the set. Secondly, how likely it is that someone could kill himself on a set that was in constant use and not be noticed by anyone – actors, directors, cameramen, grips, sound men, light operators – and then ignored by everyone who worked on the film in post-production as well.

51. Edwards, *Judy Garland*, p 63.
52. 'There'll Always Be Another Encore', *McCall's Magazine*, January/February 1964.
53. For example, it was announced that Theda Bara had been born in an oasis under the shadow of the Sphinx; that 'Bara' was 'Arab' backwards and 'Theda' was an anagram of 'death'. Newspapers began running her picture captioned 'Is This The Wickedest Face In The World?' Other stories circulated that she was the reincarnation of historical

villainesses such as Delilah and Lucrezia Borgia. In fact, she was Theodosia Goodman, the Cincinnati, Ohio-born daughter of a Polish-Jewish tailor.

54. Thomas J Watson and Bill Chapman, *Judy Portrait of a Legend* (McGraw Hill: New York, 1986) p 26.

55. It was not a happy marriage. The couple separated on 17 March 1943 and were divorced on 2 August 1945.

56. 'Who Said "The Terrible Teens"?', James Reid, *Motion Picture*, May 1940.

57. Edwards, *Judy Garland*, p 82.

58. The play on which this film was based opened in New York City on 13 November 1922 and ran for 248 performances. However, most of the plot and all but two of the songs were replaced for the cinematic version. In one scene Judy sings *Singin' in the Rain*, ten years before Gene Kelly made it famous. This is also the only film in which Judy dies on-screen.

59. Frank, *Judy*, p 159.

60. The Ambassador Hotel at 3400 Wilshire Boulevard opened on 1 January 1921. It quickly became one of Hollywood's in places. Some months after the hotel opened its nightclub The Cocoanut Grove opened and was the most glamorous venue in the area. The Oscars were held at the Grove in 1930, 1940 and 1943. The Grove was used as a location for Judy's 1954 film *A Star Is Born*. Marilyn Monroe's first modelling agent, Emmeline Snively, had offices in the Ambassador. On 5 June 1958 Senator Bobby Kennedy was assassinated in the basement kitchen while running for the presidency. The Ambassador closed in 1989 and was demolished on 16 January 2006.

61. This was the first film in which Judy's name appeared above the title.

62. Edwards, *Judy Garland*, p 90.

63. Edwards, *Judy Garland*, p 90.

64. David Shipman, *Judy Garland* (Fourth Estate, London: 1992) p 135.

65. Clarke, *Get Happy*, p 160.

66. Born in 1917, she eventually committed suicide.

67. Shipman, *Judy Garland*, p 135.

68. Frank, *Judy*, p 150.

69. Clarke, *Get Happy*, p 168.

70. Edwards, *Judy Garland*, p 92.

71. Edwards, *Judy Garland*, p 93.

72. Edwards, *Judy Garland*, p 95.

73. During the *Trolley* song one of the extras shouts 'Hi, Judy'. Judy is playing a character called Esther. When Esther dances with her little sister Tootie (Margaret O'Brien) the younger girl is wearing pink slippers but later they turn blue.

74. Paul Donnelley, *Fade to Black* (Omnibus, London and New York: 2005) p 946.

75. The Villa Nova was also the setting for the blind date between Marilyn Monroe and Joe Di Maggio in March 1952. It is now The Rainbow Grill and tends not to attract Hollywood stars anymore.

76. Edwards, *Judy Garland*, p 104.

77. Edwards, *Judy Garland*, p 107.

78. Edwards, *Judy Garland*, p 108.

79. He died on 11 November 1947.

80. Edwards, *Judy Garland*, p 110.

81. 'There'll Always Be Another Encore', *McCall's Magazine*, January/February 1964.

82. There'll Always Be Another Encore', *McCall's Magazine*, January/February 1964.

83. There'll Always Be Another Encore', *McCall's Magazine*, January/February 1964.

84. Edwards, *Judy Garland*, p 118.

85. Now the Austen Riggs Centre.

86. Congressman J Parnell Thomas headed the House Un-American Activities Committee in Washington. Among the committee members was Richard M Nixon. Thomas was a publicity-seeker and realised that scalps of suspected Communists or fellow travellers in Hollywood would garner him far more publicity than those uncovered in Washington. John Huston, William Wyler and Philip Dunne formed an organisation called 'Hollywood Fights Back', later renamed the Committee for the First Amendment, to attempt to counter what was happening in Washington. Present at one of the first meetings were Humphrey Bogart and Betty Bacall, Huston, Wyler, Dunne, Edward G Robinson, Billy Wilder, Gene Kelly, Danny Kaye, Burt Lancaster, Judy and Vincente Minnelli. Several of the attendees, but not Judy or Minnelli, later flew to Washington in an aeroplane donated by Howard Hughes to continue their protest.

87. Edwards, *Judy Garland*, p 117.

88. The role of Nadine Hale was originally to be played by Cyd Charisse but she broke her leg and had to withdraw. Miller was not much fitter and had a bad back during filming and only made it through with copious use of

painkillers. She also wore ballet shoes and flattened her hairstyle so as not to dwarf Astaire in their duet scenes.

89. Frank, *Judy*, p 299.
90. It was remade again as *You've Got Mail* (1998) starring Tom Hanks and Meg Ryan.
91. The event was so traumatic that it led to her appearing in *A Child Is Waiting* (1962), opposite Burt Lancaster, for John Cassavetes as a teacher in a school for the backward.
92. Frank, *Judy*, p 265.
93. Frank, *Judy*, p 265.
94. The film star Clint Eastwood was elected mayor of Carmel in 1986.
95. Donnelley, *Fade to Black*, p 395.
96. Edwards, *Judy Garland*, p 133.
97. Clarke, *Get Happy*, p 272.
98. Edwards, *Judy Garland*, p 135.
99. *Modern Screen*, November 1950.
100. By this time Sue had married the bandleader Jack Cathcart and was living in Las Vegas, Nevada, while Jimmy was residing in Dallas with her husband Thomas Thompson.
101. *Modern Screen*, May 1951.
102. Edwards, *Judy Garland*, pp 150–1.
103. Edwards, *Judy Garland*, p 152.
104. *The Guardian*, 19 September 2005.
105. *The Independent*, 19 September 2005.
106. Clarke, *Get Happy*, pp 352–3
107. *The Independent*, 19 September 2005.
108. Edwards, *Judy Garland*, p 168.
109. Frank, *Judy*, p 352.
110. Edwards, *Judy Garland*, p 169.

111. Lorna Luft, *Me and My Shadows: A Family Story* (Sidgwick & Jackson, London: 1998) p 58.

112. Ethel knocked three years off her age when she had her daughters and her death certificate states that she was born not in 1893 but in 1896.

113. Bowers began his film career in 1916, often working with Marguerite de la Motte, later to become his wife. His career was ended by the advent of sound and on 17 November 1936 Bowers committed suicide by rowing into the Pacific Ocean off Santa Monica and drowning himself.

114. It is not often that original films and remakes win Oscars. The 1937 and 1976 versions of *A Star Is Born* both won an Oscar (in 1976 *Evergreen* won for Best Song) but Judy's version went home empty-handed.

115. Frank, *Judy*, p 382.

116. Peter Harry Brown and Patte B Barham, *Marilyn The Last Take* (William Heineman, London: 1992) p 122.

117. Edwards, *Judy Garland*, p 177.

118. Frank, *Judy*, pp 387–8.

119. Mason Wiley and Damien Bona, *Inside Oscar* (2nd edition) (Ballantine Books, New York: 1996) p 246.

120. Wiley and Bona, *Inside Oscar*, p 246.

121. Frank, *Judy*, p 394.

122. Frank, *Judy*, p 394.

123. Edwards, *Judy Garland*, p 181.

124. Clarke, *Get Happy*, p 344.

125. Edwards, *Judy Garland*, p 182.

126. Edwards, *Judy Garland*, p 181.

127. Edwards, *Judy Garland*, p 185.

128. The Voice of Broadway column in the *New York Journal-American*, 14 January 1959.

129. Edwards, *Judy Garland*, pp 187–8.
130. Frank, *Judy*, p 471.
131. Edwards, *Judy Garland*, p 192.
132. *New York Herald Tribune*, 24 April 1961.
133. Simon Rose, *Simon Rose's Classic Film Guide* (HarperCollins, London: 1995) p 193.
134. *Variety*, 18 October 1961.
135. Edwards, *Judy Garland*, p 196.
136. Another nominee, Audrey Hepburn, was also in the hotel. She had flown in from Switzerland to attend but fell ill with a sore throat and was confined to bed.
137. John F Kennedy International Airport since 24 December 1963.
138. 'The Plot Against Judy Garland', *Ladies Home Journal*, August 1967.
139. 'The Plot Against Judy Garland', *Ladies Home Journal*, August 1967.
140. Al Di Orio, *Little Girl Lost The Life & Hard Times Of Judy Garland* (Robson Books, London: 1975), pp 282–7.
141. *New York Times* 30 September 1963.
142. Di Orio, *Little Girl Lost*, p 163.
143. Di Orio, *Little Girl Lost*, p 165.
144. Di Orio, *Little Girl Lost*, p 164.
145. Di Orio, *Little Girl Lost*, p 168.
146. The other stars included: Eve Arden, Jane Asher, Richard Attenborough, Dora Bryan, Max Bygraves, Adrienne Corri, Wendy Craig, Peggy Cummins, Angela Douglas, Dame Edith Evans, Zsa Zsa Gabor, Joyce Grenfell, Susan Hampshire, Frankie Howerd, Miriam Karlin, Millicent Martin, Hayley Mills, Rita Moreno, Sir Laurence Olivier,

Chita Rivera, Harry Secombe, Marti Stevens, Sylvia Syms, Frankie Vaughan, Elisabeth Welch and Barbara Windsor.

147. George Mair, *Under the Rainbow: The Real Liza Minnelli* (Aurum, London: 1997), p 4.

148. Wendy Leigh, *Liza* (Dutton, New York: 1993) p 80.

149. Di Orio, *Little Girl Lost*, p 194.

150. Di Orio, *Little Girl Lost*, p 198.

151. Ironically the character of drug-taking Neely O'Hara was based on the young Judy.

152. Edwards, *Judy Garland*, p 238.

153. Edwards, *Judy Garland*, p 239.

154. Iain Calder, *The Untold Story: My 20 Years Running the National Enquirer* (Hyperion, New York: 2004) pp 50–1.

Filmography

Key: MGM = Metro-Goldwyn-Mayer; TCF = Twentieth Century-Fox; WB = Warner Bros; C = Columbia; UA = United Artists.

Starlet Revue (Mayfair Pictures Corporation) Cast: JUDY GARLAND (Frances Gumm) as herself; Mary Jane Gumm as herself; Virginia Gumm as herself. Released: 1929.

A Holiday in Storyland (Warner Bros Vitaphone) Director: Roy Mack. Cast: The Gumm Sisters. Released: 1930.

The Wedding of Jack and Jill (Warner Bros Vitaphone) Director: Roy Mack. Cast: Johnnie Pirone, Jr as Jack; Peggy Ryan as Jill; The Gumm Sisters. Released: June 1930.

Bubbles (Warner Bros Vitaphone) Director: Roy Mack. Cast: The Vitaphone Kiddies; The Gumm Sisters; Mae Questel as mother. Released: 1930.

La Fiesta de Santa Barbara (MGM) Director: Louis Lewyn. Cast: Eduardo Durant's Fiesta Orchestra as themselves; The

Spanish Troubadors as themselves; Warner Baxter as himself;
Ralph Forbes as himself; The Fanchonettes as themselves; The
Garland Sisters as themselves; Kirby and DeGage as themselves;
Dude Ranch Wranglers as themselves; Chester Conklin as
himself; Mary Carlisle as herself; Cecilia Parker as herself;
Shirley Ross as herself; Rosalind Keith as herself; Ida Lupino as
herself; Toby Wing as herself. Released: 7 December 1935.
NOTES: This was the last time that the Garland Sisters ever
appeared together.

Every Sunday (MGM) Director: Felix E Feist. Producer: Jack
Chertok. Cast: JUDY GARLAND (Judy); Deanna Durbin
(Edna). Released: 1936.
NOTES: Judy is called 'Judy' in the film but Deanna is referred
to by her real name, Edna.
SONGS: *America*, *Opera vs Jazz*, *Waltz in Springtime*.

Pigskin Parade (TCF) Director: David Butler. Producer:
Bogart Rogers. Screenplay: Harry Tugend. Cast: Stuart Erwin
as Amos Dodd; Patsy Kelly as Bessie Winters; Jack Haley as
Winston 'Slug' Winters; Johnny Downs as Chip Carson; Betty
Grable as Laura Watson; Arline Judge as Sally Saxon; Dixie
Dunbar as Ginger Jones; JUDY GARLAND as Sairy Dodd;
Fred Kohler Jr as Biff Bentley; Grady Sutton as Mortimer
Higgins; Elisha Cook Jr as Herbert Terwilliger Van Dyck;
Edward J Nugent as Sparks; Julius Tannen as Dr Burke; Tony
Martin as Tommy Barker; Eddie Nugent as Sparks; Sam
Hayes as Radio Announcer at ballgame; Bob McClung as
Country Boy; George Herbert as the professor; Jack Murphy
as the usher; Pat Flaherty as the referee; David Sharpe as the
messenger boy; Si Jenks as the baggage master; John Dilson as

the doctor; Jack Stoney as a policeman; George Y Harvey as the brakeman; Ben Hall as a boy in the stadium; Lynn Bari as a girl in the stadium; Charles Wilson as Yale's coach; George Offerman Jr as Freddy; Maurice Cass as Professor Tutweiler; Jack Best as Professor McCormick; Douglas Wood as Professor Dutton; Charles Croker-King as Professor Pillsbury; Alan Ladd as a student; Edward Le Saint as the judge; Jed Prouty as Mr Van Dyke; Emma Dunn as Mrs Van Dyke. Released: 23 October 1936.

SONGS: *It's Love I'm After*, *The Texas Tornado*, *The Balboa* (*Hold That Bulldog* not used).

Broadway Melody Of 1938 (MGM) Director: Roy Del Ruth. Producer: Jack Cummings. Cast: Robert Taylor as Steve Raleigh; Eleanor Powell as Sally Lee; George Murphy as Sonny Ledford; Binnie Barnes as Caroline Whipple; Buddy Ebsen as Peter Trot; Sophie Tucker as Alice Clayton; JUDY GARLAND as Betty Clayton; Charles Igor Gorin as Nicki Papaloopas; Raymond Walburn as Herman J Whipple; Robert Benchley as Duffy; Willie Howard as a waiter; Charley Grapewin as James K Blakeley; Robert Wildhack as the sneezer; Billy Gilbert as George Papaloopas; Barnett Parker as Jerry Jason. Released: 20 August 1937.

SONGS: *(Dear Mr Gable) You Made Me Love You*, *Everybody Sing*, *Yours and Mine*.

Thoroughbreds Don't Cry (MGM) Director: Alfred E Green. Producer: Harry Rapf. Cast: Ronald Sinclair as Roger Calverton; JUDY GARLAND as Cricket West; Mickey Rooney as Tim Donovan; C Aubrey Smith as Sir Peter Calverton; Sophie Tucker as Mother 'Aunt Edie' Ralph; Forrester Harvey as Mr Wilkins; Charles D Brown as 'Click' Donovan; Frankie Darro as 'Dink' Reid; Henry Kolker as 'Doc' Godfrey; Helen Troy as Hilda. Released: 25 November 1937.

SONGS: *Gotta Pair of New Shoes*, *Sun Showers* (recorded but not used).

Everybody Sing (MGM) Director: Edwin L Marin. Producer: Harry Rapf. Cast: Allan Jones as Ricky Saboni; JUDY GARLAND as Judy Bellaire; Fanny Brice as Olga Chekaloff; Reginald Owen as Hillary Bellaire; Billie Burke as Diana Bellaire; Reginald Gardiner as Jerrold Hope; Lynne Carver as Sylvia Bellaire; Helen Troy as Hillary's secretary; Monty Woolley as Jack Fleming; Adia Kuznetzoff as Boris the bus driver; Henry Armetta as Giovanni Vittorino; Michelette Burani as Madame Le Brouchette; Mary Forbes as Miss Colvin. Released: 4 February 1938.

SONGS: *Sweet Chariot*, *Down on Melody Farm*, *Swing Mr Mendelssohn*, *Why? Because*, bus sequence.

Love Finds Andy Hardy (MGM) Director: George B Seitz. Producers: Lou L Ostrow and Carey Wilson. Cast: Mickey Rooney as Andy Hardy; Lewis Stone as Judge James K Hardy; Fay Holden as Emily Hardy; Cecilia Parker as Marian Hardy; JUDY GARLAND as Betsy Booth; Lana Turner as Cynthia Potter; Ann Rutherford as Polly Benedict; Mary Howard as Mary Tompkins; Gene Reynolds as Jimmy MacMahon, Jr; Don Castle as Dennis Hunt; Betty Ross Clarke as Aunt Millie Forrest; Marie Blake as Augusta; George P Breakston as Francis Bacon 'Beezy' Anderson; Raymond Hatton as Peter Dugan; Frank Darien as Mr. Barnes. Released: 22 July 1938.

SONGS: *Meet the Beat of My Heart*, *In Between*, *It Never Rains*

But What It Pours (not used), *Bei Mir Bist Du Schoen* (not used).

Listen Darling (MGM) Director: Edwin L Marin. Producer: Jack Cummings. Cast: JUDY GARLAND as 'Pinkie' Wingate; Freddie Bartholomew as Herbert 'Buzz' Mitchell; Mary Astor as Dottie Wingate; Walter Pidgeon as Richard Thurlow; Alan Hale as J J Slattery; Scotty Beckett as Billie Wingate; Barnett Parker as Abercrombie; Gene Lockhart as Arthur Drubbs; Charley Grapewin as Uncle Joe Higgins. Première: 18 October 1938.
NOTES: This was Judy's sixth feature film but the first in which she received top billing.
SONGS: *Ten Pins in the Sky, Zing! Went the Strings of My Heart, On the Bumpy Road to Love.*

The Wizard of Oz (MGM) Director: Victor Fleming. Producer: Mervyn LeRoy. Cast: JUDY GARLAND as Dorothy Gale; Frank Morgan as Professor Marvel/Emerald City doorman/The cabbie/The Wizard's guard/The Wizard of Oz; Ray Bolger as Hunk/The Scarecrow; Bert Lahr as Zeke/The Cowardly Lion; Jack Haley as Hickory/The Tin Man; Billie Burke as Glinda, the Good Witch of the North; Margaret Hamilton as Miss Gulch/The Wicked Witch of the West/The Wicked Witch of the East; Charley Grapewin as Uncle Henry; Pat Walshe as Nikko; Clara Blandick as Auntie Em; Terry as Toto. Première: 12 August 1939.
NOTES: MGM paid $75,000 for the film rights.
—Humorist Ogden Nash wrote an unused screenplay.
—The film was known at MGM as Production No 1060.
—According to Jerry Maren, the Munchkins were paid $50 per

week for a six-day working week, while Terry as Toto the dog received $125 per week.

—The singing voice of Jack Haley was provided by Buddy Ebsen.

—The tornado was a 35-foot-long muslin stocking, photographed with Kansas farms and fields in miniature.

—*The Wizard of Oz* took 22 weeks to film, involved 65 sets and 600 performers.

—The music was played by a 160-piece orchestra.

—The first television showing of *The Wizard of Oz* was on CBS on 3 November 1956.

—The line 'Toto, I don't think we're in Kansas anymore' is often used to open Village People concerts.

SONGS: *Somewhere Over the Rainbow, Follow the Yellow Brick Road, We're Off to See the Wizard, Munchkinland, The Jitterbug* (not used).

Babes In Arms (MGM) Director: Busby Berkeley. Producer: Arthur Freed. Cast: Mickey Rooney as Mickey Moran; JUDY GARLAND as Patsy Barton; Charles Winninger as Joe Moran; Guy Kibbee as Judge John Black; June Preisser as Rosalie Essex; Grace Hayes as Florrie Moran; Betty Jaynes as Molly Moran; Douglas McPhail as Don Brice; Rand Brooks as Jeff Steele; Leni Lynn as Dody Martin; Johnny Sheffield as Bobs; Henry Hull as Maddox; Barnett Parker as William Bartlett; Ann Shoemaker as Mrs Barton; Margaret Hamilton as Martha Steele. Première: 10 October 1939.

NOTES: Rooney received an Oscar nomination for Best Actor.

SONGS: *I Cried for You, Good Morning, Where or When, God's Country, Opera vs Jazz.*

Andy Hardy Meets Debutante (MGM) Director: George B Seitz. Producer: J J Cohn. Cast: Mickey Rooney as Andy Hardy; Lewis Stone as Judge James K Hardy; Fay Holden as Emily Hardy; Cecilia Parker as Marian Hardy; JUDY GARLAND as Betsy Booth; Ann Rutherford as Polly Benedict; Diana Lewis as Daphne Fowler; George P Breakston as F Baker 'Beezy' Anderson; Sara Haden as Aunt Milly Forrest; Addison Richards as George Benedict; George Lessey as Underwood; Cy Kendall as Mr Carrillo; Clyde Willson as Francis aka Butch. Released: 5 July 1940.
SONGS: *I'm Nobody's Baby, Alone, Buds Won't Bud* (not used), *All I Do is Dream of You* (not used).

Strike Up The Band (MGM) Director: Busby Berkeley. Producer: Arthur Freed. Cast: Mickey Rooney as Jimmy Connors; JUDY GARLAND as Mary Holden; Paul Whiteman and Orchestra as themselves; June Preisser as Barbara Frances Morgan; William Tracy as Phil Turner; Larry Nunn as Willie Brewster; Margaret Early as Annie; Ann Shoemaker as Jessie Connors; Francis Pierlot as Mr Judd; Virginia Brissac as Mrs May Holden; George Lessey as Mr Morgan; Enid Bennett as Mrs Morgan; Howard C Hickman as Doctor; Sarah Edwards as Miss Hodges. Released: 27 September 1940.
SONGS: *Nobody, Drummer Boy, Do the la Conga, Nell of New Rochelle, Our Love Affair, Finale.*

Little Nellie Kelly (MGM) Director: Norman Taurog. Producer: Arthur Freed. Cast: JUDY GARLAND as Nellie Kelly/Little Nellie Kelly; George Murphy as Jerry Kelly; Charles Winninger as Mike Noonan; Douglas McPhail as Dennis Fogarty; Arthur Shields as Timothy Fogarty; Rita Page as Mary

Fogarty; Forrester Harvey as Moriarity; James Burke as Police Sergeant McGowan; George Watts as Mr Keevan. Released: 22 November 1940.

SONGS: *A Pretty Girl Milking her Cow, Singin' In the Rain, It's a Great Day for the Irish, Nellie Kelly I Love You, Danny Boy* (not used).

Ziegfeld Girl (MGM) Director: Robert Z Leonard. Producer: Pandro S Berman. Cast: James Stewart as Gil Young; JUDY GARLAND as Susan Gallagher; Hedy Lamarr as Mrs Sondra Kolter; Lana Turner as Sheila Regan; Tony Martin as Frank Merton; Jackie Cooper as Jerry Regan; Ian Hunter as Geoffrey Collis; Charles Winninger as Ed 'Pop' Gallagher; Edward Everett Horton as Nobel Sage; Philip Dorn as Franz Kolter; Paul Kelly as John Slayton; Antonio as speciality act dancer in *Minnie from Trinidad* number; Rosario as speciality act dancer in *Minnie from Trinidad* number; Eve Arden as Patsy Dixon; Dan Dailey as Jimmy Walters. Released: 25 April 1941.

SONGS: *Minnie from Trinidad, Ziegfeld Girl, Laugh? I Thought I'd Split My Sides, I'm Always Chasing Rainbows, Finale.*

Life Begins for Andy Hardy (MGM) Director/Producer: George B Seitz. Cast: Lewis Stone as Judge James K Hardy; Mickey Rooney as Andy Hardy; Fay Holden as Emily Hardy; Ann Rutherford as Polly Benedict; Sara Haden as Aunt Milly Forrest; Patricia Dane as Jennitt Hicks; Ray McDonald as Jimmy Frobisher; JUDY GARLAND as Betsy Booth. Released: 15 August 1941.

SONGS: *Easy to Love, Abide with Me, The Rosary, America* (none used).

Babes on Broadway (MGM) Director: Busby Berkeley.
Producer: Arthur Freed. Cast: Mickey Rooney as Tom
Williams; JUDY GARLAND as Penny Morris; Fay Bainter as
Miss Jones; Virginia Weidler as Barbara Josephine Conway;
Ray McDonald as Ray Lambert; Richard Quine as Morton
'Hammy' Hammond; Donald Meek as Mr Stone; Alexander
Woollcott as himself; Luis Alberni as Nick; James Gleason
as Thornton Reed; Emma Dunn as Mrs Williams; Frederick
Burton as Theodore Morris; Cliff Clark as Inspector Moriarity;
William Post Jr as Woollcott's announcer. Released: 31
December 1941.
SONGS: *Mary's a Grand Old Name, Rings on My Fingers, How
About You?, Chin Up Cheerio Carry On, Bombshell from Brazil,
Hoe Down, Minstrel Show.*

For Me and My Gal (MGM) Director: Busby Berkeley.
Producer: Arthur Freed. Cast: JUDY GARLAND as Jo
Hayden; George Murphy as Jimmy K Metcalf; Gene Kelly as
Harry Palmer; Mártha Eggerth as Eve Minard; Ben Blue as Sid
Simms; Stephen McNally as Mr Waring. Released: 21 October
1942.
SONGS: *After You're Gone, How Ya Gonna Keep 'Em Down on the
Farm, Ballin' the Jack, Where Do We Go from Here Boys?, For Me
and My Gal, Oh You Beautiful Doll,* First World War medley.

Presenting Lily Mars (MGM) Director: Norman Taurog.
Producer: Joseph Ruttenberg. Cast: JUDY GARLAND as
Lily Mars; Van Heflin as John Thornway; Fay Bainter as Mimi
Thornway; Richard Carlson as Owen Vail; Spring Byington
as Mrs Flora Mars; Mártha Eggerth as Isabel Rekay; Connie
Gilchrist as Frankie; Leonid Kinskey as Leo; Patricia Barker

as Poppy Mars; Janet Chapman as Rosie Mars; Annie Ross as
Violet Mars; Douglas Croft as Davey Mars; Ray McDonald
as Charlie Potter; Tommy Dorsey and His Orchestra as
themselves; Bob Crosby Orchestra as themselves. Released: 29
April 1943.
SONGS: *When I Look At You, Tom Tom the Piper's Son, Every
Little Movement, Finale, Caro Mono* (not used), *Paging Mr
Greenback* (not used).

Girl Crazy (MGM) Directors: Busby Berkeley and Norman
Taurog. Producer: Arthur Freed. Cast: Mickey Rooney as
Danny Churchill, Jr; JUDY GARLAND as Ginger Gray; Gil
Stratton as Bud Livermore; Robert E Strickland as Henry
Lathrop; Rags Ragland as 'Rags'; June Allyson as speciality
act singer; Nancy Walker as Polly Williams; Guy Kibbee as
Dean Phineas Armour; Tommy Dorsey & His Orchestra as
themselves, Charles Walters as a dancer; Frances Rafferty as
Marjorie Tait, Henry O'Neill as Danny Churchill, Sr, Howard
Freeman as Governor Tait. Released: 26 November 1943.
SONGS: *But Not For Me, Boy What Love Has Done for Me, I Got
Rhythm, Embraceable You, Bidin' My Time.*

As Thousands Cheer (MGM) Director: George Sidney.
Producer: Joe Pasternak. Cast: Kathryn Grayson as Kathryn
Jones; Gene Kelly as Private Eddie Marsh; Mary Astor as
Hyllary Jones; John Boles as Colonel Bill Jones; Ben Blue as
Chuck Polansky; Frances Rafferty as Marie Corbino; Mary
Elliott as Helen Corbino; Frank Jenks as Sergeant Koslack;
Frank Sully as Alan; Dick Simmons as Captain Fred Avery;
Ben Lessy as Silent Monk; Mickey Rooney as himself; JUDY
GARLAND as herself; Red Skelton as himself; Eleanor Powell

as herself. Released: 13 September 1943.
SONG: *The Joint is Really Jumpin' Down at Carnegie Hall.*

Meet Me in St Louis (MGM) Director: Vincente Minnelli.
Producer: Arthur Freed. Cast: JUDY GARLAND as Esther
Smith; Margaret O'Brien as 'Tootie' Smith; Mary Astor as
Mrs Anna Smith; Lucille Bremer as Rose Smith; Leon Ames
as Alonzo Smith; Tom Drake as John Truett; Marjorie Main as
Katie; Harry Davenport as Grandpa; June Lockhart as Lucille
Ballard; Henry H Daniels Jr as Alonzo Smith Jr; Joan Carroll
as Agnes Smith; Hugh Marlowe as Colonel Darly; Robert Sully
as Warren Sheffield; Chill Wills as Mr. Neely; Gary Gray as the
boy at the pavilion. Released: 22 November 1944.
SONGS: *The Boy Next Door, Have Yourself a Merry Little
Christmas, The Trolley Song, Skip to My Lou, Over the Bannister,
Meet Me in St Louis, Boys and Girls Like You and Me* (not used).
NOTES: Between takes Margaret O'Brien would often
re-arrange the props, much to the annoyance of the crew.
—Leon Ames's singing voice was dubbed.

The Clock (MGM) Director: Vincente Minnelli. Producer:
Arthur Freed. Cast: JUDY GARLAND as Alice Mayberry;
Robert Walker as Corporal Joe Allen; James Gleason as Al
Henry; Keenan Wynn as cafeteria drunk; Marshall Thompson
as Bill; Lucile Gleason as Mrs Al Henry; Ruth Brady as Helen.
Première: 22 March 1945.

The Harvey Girls (MGM) Director: George Sidney. Producer:
Arthur Freed. Cast: JUDY GARLAND as Susan Bradley; John
Hodiak as Ned Trent; Ray Bolger as Chris Maule; Preston
Foster as Judge Sam Purvis; Virginia O'Brien as Alma; Angela

Lansbury as Em; Marjorie Main as Sonora Cassidy; Chill Wills as H H Hartsey; Kenny Baker as Terry O'Halloran; Selena Royle as Miss Bliss; Cyd Charisse as Deborah; Ruth Brady as Ethel; Catherine McLeod as Louise; Jack Lambert as Marty Peters; Edward Earle as Jed Adams. Première: 18 January 1946. SONGS: *On the Atchison, Topeka and the Santa Fe, In the Valley When the Evening Sun Comes Down, Swing Your Partner, It's a Great Big World.*

Ziegfeld Follies of 1946 (MGM) Directors: Lemuel Ayers, Roy Del Ruth, Lemuel Ayers, Roy Del Ruth, Robert Lewis, Eugene Loring, Vincente Minnelli, George Sidney, Charles Walters, John Murray Anderson. Cast: Fred Astaire as Fred Astaire/ Raffles/Tai Long/the gentleman in *The Babbit and the Bromide*; Lucille Ball as speciality act; Lucille Bremer as Princess/Moy Ling; Fanny Brice as Norma; JUDY GARLAND as speciality act; Kathryn Grayson as speciality act; Lena Horne as speciality act; Gene Kelly as the gentleman in *The Babbit and the Bromide*; James Melton as Alfredo in scene from *La Traviata*; Victor Moore as Lawyer's client; Red Skelton as Announcer/J Newton Numbskull; Esther Williams as speciality act; William Powell as Florenz Ziegfeld Jr; Edward Arnold as Lawyer; Marion Bell as Violetta in scene from *La Traviata*. Released: 22 March 1946.

Till the Clouds Roll By (MGM) Director: Richard Whorf. Cast: June Allyson as Jane in *Leave it to Jane*/speciality act; Lucille Bremer as Sally Hessler; JUDY GARLAND as Marilyn Miller; Kathryn Grayson as Magnolia in *Show Boat*/speciality act; Van Heflin as James I Hessler; Lena Horne as Julie in *Show Boat*/speciality act; Van Johnson as the bandleader in Elite

Club; Tony Martin as Gaylord Ravenal in *Show Boat*/speciality act; Dinah Shore as speciality act; Frank Sinatra as Finale speciality act; Robert Walker as Jerome Kern; Gower Champion as speciality act in *Roberta*; Cyd Charisse as dance speciality act in *Roberta*; Harry Hayden as Charles Frohman; Paul Langton as Oscar Hammerstein. Released: 5 December 1946.
SONGS: *Who?*, *Look for the Silver Lining*.

The Pirate (MGM) Director: Vincente Minnelli. Producer: Arthur Freed. Cast: JUDY GARLAND as Manuela; Gene Kelly as Serafin; Walter Slezak as Don Pedro Vargas; Gladys Cooper as Aunt Inez; Reginald Owen as The Advocate; George Zucco as The Viceroy; The Nicholas Brothers as speciality act dance; Fayard Nicholas as speciality act dance; Lester Allen as Uncle Capucho; Harold Nicholas as speciality act dance; Lola Deem as Isabella; Ellen Ross as Mercedes; Mary Jo Ellis as Lizarda; Jean Dean as Casilda; Marion Murray as Eloise. Released: 20 May 1948.
SONGS: *Love of My Life*, *Mack the Black*, *You Can Do No Wrong*, *Be a Clown*, *Voodoo* (not used).
NOTES: *The Pirate* was Judy's only MGM picture to lose money. —Cole Porter hated the film calling it 'a $5,000,000 Hollywood picture that was unspeakably wretched, the worst that money could buy'.

Easter Parade (MGM) Director: Charles Walters. Producer: Arthur Freed. Cast: JUDY GARLAND as Hannah Brown; Fred Astaire as Don Hewes; Peter Lawford as Jonathan Harrow III; Ann Miller as Nadine Hale; Jules Munshin as François; Clinton Sundberg as Mike the barman; Richard Beavers as a singer. Released: 30 June 1948.

SONGS: *A Fella with an Umbrella, It Only Happens When I Dance with You, Better Luck Next Time, A Couple of Swells, I Want to Go Back to Michigan,* Medley: *I Love a Piano/ When the Midnight Choo-Choo Leaves for Alabam/ Snooky Ookums, Mr Monotony* (not used).

NOTES: Roger Edens and Johnny Green won an Academy Award for Best Scoring of a Musical Picture.

Words and Music (MGM) Director: Norman Taurog. Producer: Arthur Freed. Cast: June Allyson as herself; Perry Como as Eddie Lorrison Anders; JUDY GARLAND as herself; Lena Horne as herself; Gene Kelly as himself; Mickey Rooney as Lorenz Hart; Ann Sothern as Joyce Harmon; Tom Drake as Richard Rodgers; Cyd Charisse as Margo Grant; Betty Garrett as Peggy Lorgan McNeil; Janet Leigh as Dorothy Feiner Rodgers; Marshall Thompson as Herbert Fields; Mel Tormé as himself; Vera-Ellen as herself; Jeanette Nolan as Mrs Hart. Released: 9 December 1948.

SONGS: *I Wish I Were in Love Again, Johnny One Note.*

NOTES: The song *I Wish I Were In Love Again* was the last time that Judy and Mickey Rooney appeared on screen together.

In the Good Old Summertime (MGM) Director: Robert Z Leonard. Producer: Harry Stradling. Cast: JUDY GARLAND as Veronica Fisher; Van Johnson as Andrew; Delby Larkin/ narrator; S Z Sakall as Otto Oberkugen; Spring Byington as Nellie Burke; Clinton Sundberg as Rudy Hansen; Buster Keaton as Hickey; Marcia Van Dyke as Louise Parkson; Lillian Bronson as Aunt Addie. Released: 29 July 1949.

SONGS: *Merry Christmas, Meet Me Tonight in Dreamland, I Don't Care, In the Good Old Summertime, Put Your Arms Around*

Me, Play that Barbershop Chord, Last Night When We Were Young
(not used).

Summer Stock (MGM) Director: Charles Walters. Producer:
Joe Pasternak. Cast: JUDY GARLAND as Jane Falbury; Gene
Kelly as Joe D Ross; Eddie Bracken as Orville Wingait; Gloria
DeHaven as Abigail Falbury; Marjorie Main as Esme; Phil
Silvers as Herb Blake; Ray Collins as Jasper G Wingait; Nita
Bieber as Sarah Higgins; Carleton Carpenter as Artie; Hans
Conried as Harrison I Keath. Released: 31 August 1950.
SONGS: *Friendly Star, If You Feel Like Singing, Sing, Happy
Harvest, You Wonderful You, All for You, Get Happy.*

A Star Is Born (WB) Director: George Cukor. Producer:
Sid Luft. Cast: JUDY GARLAND as Esther Blodgett/Vicki
Lester; James Mason as Norman Maine; Jack Carson as Matt
Libby; Charles Bickford as Oliver Niles; Tommy Noonan as
Danny McGuire; Lucy Marlow as Lola Lavery; Amanda Blake
as Susan Ettinger; Irving Bacon as Graves; Hazel Shermet as
Libby's secretary; Lotus Robb as Miss Markham. Première: 29
September 1954.
SONGS: *The Man That Got Away, Gotta Have Me Go with You,
Here's What I'm Here For, It's a New World, Someone at Last, Lose
that Long Face, Born in a Trunk.*
NOTES: This was the third version of the story to reach the
screen. The first was *What Price Hollywood?* (1932) which was
directed by George Cukor and the second was *A Star is Born*
(1937). A fourth version, also entitled *A Star is Born*, was
released in 1976.
—James Mason based the character of the alcoholic Norman
Maine on some alcoholic friends, not John Barrymore as

George Cukor had suggested.

—The film was originally released at 181 minutes but Jack Warner ordered the excision of 27 minutes a week after the première. The lost footage included the song *Here What's I'm Here For* performed by Judy and a sequence where Norman Maine asks Esther to marry him.

—Cukor refused to watch the cut version of the film. He relented in 1983 when it was restored but died before he had the chance to view it. The restored version was premièred in July 1983 at the Radio City Music Hall, 1260 Avenue of the Americas in New York.

Pepe (C) Director/Producer: George Sidney. Cast: Cantinflas as Pepe; Dan Dailey as Ted Holt; Shirley Jones as Suzie Murphy; Carlos Montalbán as Rodriguez; Vicki Trickett as Lupita; Matt Mattox as Dancer; Hank Henry as Manager; Suzanne Lloyd as Carmen; Carlos Rivas in a cameo appearance; Maurice Chevalier in a cameo appearance; Bing Crosby in a cameo appearance; Michael Callan as dancer; Richard Conte in a cameo appearance; Bobby Darin in a cameo appearance; Sammy Davis Jr in a cameo appearance; Jimmy Durante in a cameo appearance; Zsa Zsa Gabor in a cameo appearance; JUDY GARLAND in a cameo appearance; Greer Garson in a cameo appearance; Joey Bishop in a cameo appearance; Hedda Hopper in a cameo appearance; Ernie Kovacs in a cameo appearance; Peter Lawford in a cameo appearance; Janet Leigh in a cameo appearance; Jack Lemmon in a cameo appearance. Released: 21 December 1960.
SONG: *The Far Away Part of Town*.

Judgment at Nuremberg (UA) Director/Producer: Stanley Kramer. Cast: Spencer Tracy as Chief Judge Dan Haywood; Burt Lancaster as Dr Ernst Janning; Richard Widmark as Colonel Tad Lawson; Marlene Dietrich as Mrs Bertholt; Maximilian Schell as Hans Rolfe; JUDY GARLAND as Irene Hoffman Wallner; Montgomery Clift as Rudolph Petersen; Ed Binns as Senator Burkette; Werner Klemperer as Emil Hahn; Torben Meyer as Werner Lampe; Martin Brandt as Friedrich Hofstetter; William Shatner as Captain Harrison Byers; Kenneth MacKenna as Judge Kenneth Norris; Alan Baxter as Brigadier General Matt Merrin; Ray Teal as Judge Curtiss Ives. Released: 19 December 1961.
NOTES: Marlene Dietrich accepted the role before she had read the script and chose her own wardrobe. It was her last major screen role.

Gay Purr-ee (WB) Director: Abe Levitow. Producer: Henry G Saperstein. Cast: JUDY GARLAND as Mewsette; Robert Goulet as Jaune-Tom; Red Buttons as Robespierre; Paul Frees as Meowrice; Hermione Gingold as Madame Rubens-Chatte. Released: 24 October 1962.
SONGS: *Take My Hand, Paree, Paris is a Lonely Town, Roses Red, Violets Blue, Little Drops of Rain, Mewsette Finale.*

A Child Is Waiting (UA) Director: John Cassavetes. Producer: Stanley Kramer. Cast: Burt Lancaster as Dr Ben Clark; JUDY GARLAND as Jean Hansen; Gena Rowlands as Sophie Widdicombe/Benham; Steven Hill as Ted Widdicombe; Paul Stewart as Goodman; Gloria McGehee as Mattie; Lawrence Tierney as Douglas Benham; Bruce Ritchey as Reuben Widdicombe; John Marley as Holland; Bill

Mumy as boy; Elizabeth Wilson as Miss Fogarty. Released: 13 February 1963.

I Could Go On Singing (UA) Director: Ronald Neame. Producer: Saul Chaplin. Cast: JUDY GARLAND as Jenny Bowman; Dirk Bogarde as David Donne; Jack Klugman as George; Aline MacMahon as Ida; Gregory Phillips as Matt; Russell Waters as Reynolds; Pauline Jameson as Miss Plimpton; Jeremy Burnham as young hospital doctor; Joey Luft as an extra on the boat; Lorna Luft as an extra on the boat. Released: 15 May 1963.
SONGS: *I Could Go On Singing, Hello Bluebird, It Never Was You, By Myself, I am the Monarch of the Sea.*

Further Reading

Autobiographies, Collections of Interviews and Family Memoirs

Luft, Lorna, *Me and My Shadows: A Family Story* (Sidgwick & Jackson, London: 1998).

Biographies

Clarke, Gerald, *Get Happy: The Life Of Judy Garland* (TimeWarner, London: 2000).

DiOrio, Jr, Al, *Little Girl Lost: The Life & Hard Times Of Judy Garland* (Robson Books, London: 1975).

Deans, Mickey with Ann Pinchot, *Weep No More My Lady: An Intimate Biography Of Judy Garland* (Mayflower, London: 1973).

Edwards, Anne, *Judy Garland* (Corgi Books, London: 1976).

Frank, Gerold, *Judy* (Da Capo, New York: 1999).

Leigh, Wendy, *Liza* (Dutton, New York: 1993).

Mair, George, *Under the Rainbow: The Real Liza Minnelli* (Aurum, London: 1997).

Meyer, John, *Heartbreaker* (Star Books, London: 1987).

Shipman, David, *Judy Garland* (Fourth Estate, London: 1992).

Other Books: Biographies and General Books on Hollywood

Calder, Iain, *The Untold Story* (Hyperion, New York: 2004).

Donnelley, Paul, *Fade to Black* (3rd edition) (Omnibus, London and New York: 2005).

Higham, Charles, *Merchant of Dreams Louis B Mayer, MGM and the Secret Hollywood* (Donald I Fine, New York: 1993).

Maltin, Leonard (ed), *Leonard Maltin's Classic Movie Guide* (Plume, New York: 2005).

Pickard, Roy, *The Oscar Movies from A-Z* (Hamlyn, London: 1982).

Wayne, Jane Ellen, *Ava's Men. The Private Life of Ava Gardner* (Robson Books, London: 1990).

Wiley, Mason and Damien Bona, *Inside Oscar* (2nd edition) (Ballantine Books, New York: 1996).

Picture Sources

The author and publisher wish to express their thanks to the following sources of illustrative material and/or permission to reproduce it. They will make proper acknowledgments in future editions in the even that any omissions have occurred.

Index

Page numbers in *italics* refer to illustrations

NB. Family relationships are to Judy Garland. For Judy Garland's films, songs, stage shows and television appearances, see under 'Garland, Judy'.